ACCOUNTABILITY AND EMPOWERMENT

THE INNER CONTROL *IS* THE TRUE CONTROL
Making Lasting Lifestyle and Behavioral Changes

BOOK 2

ACCOUNTABILITY AND EMPOWERMENT

A Four-Step Strategy for Overcoming Resentment

A. Sehatti, RN, MSN
Family Nurse Practitioner

NCWC/Amend-Health Press

ACCOUNTABILITY AND EMPOWERMENT: *A Four-Step Strategy for Overcoming Resentment* **(2) THE INNER CONTROL IS THE TRUE CONTROL:** *Making Lasting Lifestyle and Behavioral Changes.* Copyright © 2020, 2021, 2022, 2023 by A. Sehatti, RN, MSN, Family Nurse Practitioner.

All rights reserved.

No part of this book may be reproduced in whole or in part, translated, stored in a retrieval system, or transmitted, in any form or by any means such as recording, electronic, mechanical, microfilming, or otherwise, without the prior written permission of the author (A. Sehatti, RN, MSN, FNP) or NCWC/Amend-Health Press.

ISBN 978-0-578-72846-9 (paperback)

Overcoming Resentment	Anger Management	Relationships	Codependency
Behavioral and Lifestyle Changes	Weight Loss	Addiction	Alcoholism
Eating Disorders	Personal Growth	Mental Health	Total Wellness

Includes biographical references and Index

Printed and bounded in the United States of America
First Printing: August 2020
Revised April 2021, March 2022, May 2023

Published by:
NCWC/Amend-Health Press
AKA Nutritional Counseling and Weight Control Clinic
51 E. Campbell Avenue, Suite 129 - 154
Campbell, CA 95008
United States
www.NCWC-AmendHealthPress.com
www.EatActThinkHealthy.com

The Wind and the Sun
An Aesop's Fable

The Wind and the Sun plan to compete against each other to find out which one is the stronger of the two.

They select a traveler on earth as the subject of their contest; They agree that the one who could take off the traveler's coat off his back is the stronger one.

The Wind, who goes first, blows hard with all his might. However, the harder he blows, the tighter the man pulls his coat around him. Forced to surrender, the Wind dies down and allows the Sun to take over.

The Sun shines on, gently but steadily. The traveler begins to feel warm and comfortable. So, he opens the buttons of his coat one by one. As he feels safe, he takes off his coat with a sigh of relief.

The steady radiation of warmth that builds trust will effect change.

For My Beloved Daughter

A Heartfelt Thank You

To my loved ones whose modeling behaviors have impacted my life's journey in a positive way. For that, I am grateful to:

My soulmate, my beloved late husband: For his love and affection, words of wisdom, foresight, and generosity.

My sunshine, my beloved daughter: For her conscientiousness, compassion, good judgment, foresight, and generosity.

My beloved late father: For his love, affection, and sensitivity, meticulous work ethic, and love of learning.

My beloved mother: For her understanding and support, inner fortitude, patience, courage, and generosity.

My beloved oldest sister: For her conscientiousness, resilience, generosity, and intense need to take care of others.

My beloved middle sister: For her affection, sensitivity, generosity, and intense need to give to others.

About the Author

A. Sehatti is a registered nurse and family nurse practitioner. She received her bachelor's degree in nursing from University of Pennsylvania and her master's degree in nursing from University of California, Los Angeles. Aside from her clinical work at such places as Caltech Health Center, UCLA, and Stanford Medical Center, she has over forty years of experience in educating adults and children on weight management, nutrition, and total wellness. A. Sehatti is highly dedicated to making a difference in people's lives. She currently works as a nutritional consultant and health educator at a private practice that she established in 2005 in Northern California. It has been the reward of witnessing people reach their health and wellness goals that has inspired her to write her books and share the tools that have helped her clients with her readers.

Books Published by A. Sehatti

BUILDING A STRONG SENSE OF SELF
Embarking on the Journey of Change
The Inner Control Is the True Control - Book 1

THE INNER CONTROL IS THE TRUE CONTROL WORKBOOK, SECOND EDITION
Inspirational Scripts

A TOOL FOR LETTING GO OF RESENTMENT AND ANGER
Short. Straightforward. Transformative.

A WORKBOOK FOR OVERCOMING RESENTMENT
Mindfulness Scripts

A HANDBOOK FOR DEALING WITH SUGAR CRAVINGS AND DEPENDENCY
NCWC's Nutrition 101 Series

NCWC'S NUTRITION 101 WORKBOOK
NCWC's Nutrition 101 Series

21-DAY LOG BOOK FOR ACHIEVING WELLNESS GOALS
NCWC's Nutrition 101 Series

Please note that this publication is not intended to replace the services offered by a mental health professional. When needed, the assistance of an expert in the area should be sought.

The books in the series of *The Inner Control Is the True Control* were primarily written to help people reach their health goals (e.g., maintain weight loss or sobriety).

These works have achieved more than what they aimed for: In addition to helping people to make lasting lifestyle changes, they have empowered many couples to transform their relationships.

A WORD OF CAUTION: Please be informed that *Accountability and Empowerment* delivers its message in a *forthright* manner.

This approach is used to help readers break down their wall of resistance (i.e., the defense mechanism of avoidance that protects your inner wounds in the short term but makes you remain stuck and face more emotional pain in the long term).

For this reason, you may experience a short-term inner turmoil as you work through some of the chapters in this book.

> *When the bandage that covers our inner wound is removed and our vulnerable core is exposed, we will naturally experience emotional pain.*

It is when we allow ourselves to attend to our core wounds that we heal and become free to move onward and achieve our health goals—this may be why the books in the series of *The Inner Control Is the True Control* have been transformational for many people.

> *"Where you stumble, there lies your treasure."*
> —Joseph Campbell

> *"What you resist, persists."*
> —Carl Jung

> *"What you feel, you can heal."*
> —John Gray

Contents

Part I: Introduction

The Inner Control Is the True Control Series   3
About this Book   7
A Personal Note to My Readers   11
What Are Some of My Ways of Thinking, Feeling, and Behaving?   17

Part II: Genuine Accountability

Chapter 1   The Genuine Accountability Process   23
Chapter 2   Gaining Control and Reducing Stress Through the Process of Genuine Accountability   33
Chapter 3   The Four-Steps of the Genuine Accountability Process   35

Part III: Overcoming Resentment through the process of Genuine Accountability

Chapter 4   I Feel Offended   47
              A Mindfulness Script   59
Chapter 5   I Feel Annoyed   71
              Mindfulness Scripts   89
Chapter 6   I Feel Jealous   103
              A Mindfulness Script   115
Chapter 7   I Feel That I Have Been Wronged   121
              Mindfulness Scripts   145

Part IV: Conclusion

Chapter 8   A Conscientious and Empowering Mindset   169

Chapter 9   Conscientious and Empowering Inner Thoughts   175
             and Self-Talks

Appendix

Appendix 1   Assertive Communications   187

Appendix 2   Personal Boundary   189

Appendix 3   A Checklist for Making Better Choices   191

References   215

Index   217

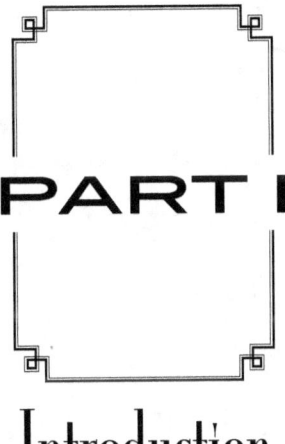

Introduction

The Inner Control Is the True Control Series

Through promoting introspection, the books in the series of *The Inner Control Is the True Control* empower readers to make lasting behavioral changes and reach a state of physical, emotional, and mental well-being (i.e., total wellness).

The first book in the series, *Building a Strong Sense of Self: Embarking on the Journey of Change,* helps people become aware of their maladaptive and limiting thought patterns that could stop them from living a healthy and fulfilled life.

This book asserts that when we remain unaware and live on autopilot, we may unconsciously respond to stressors (i.e., situations or events that cause emotional stress) based on a set of misguided principles that we have adopted in the early years of our childhood.

In such a case as this, our faulty mindset produces distorted internal thoughts and self-talks, generates negative emotions, and drives automatic and unhealthy behaviors that could hold us back from meeting our goals and reaching our full potential (Table 1 on Page 4).

Building a Strong Sense of Self concludes that when we gain awareness and cultivate a *constructive* mindset that is founded on sound principles, such as logical reasoning and self-compassion, then a set of healthy inner thoughts and self-dialogues drives our behaviors and helps us stay in control, make better choices, achieve our goals, and reach a state of total wellness (Table 2 on Page 4).

Table 1

A Misguided Mindset
I.e., *"We are defined by external factors, such as our physical attributes, accomplishments, wealth, material possessions, social status, or popularity"*
↓
Negative Internal Thoughts and Dialogues
E.g., *"I'm inadequate because I'm overweight."*
↓
Painful Emotions and Feelings
I.e., Shame and anxiety (i.e., fearing other people's judgment, rejection, and abandonment)
↓
Maladaptive Behaviors and Coping Mechanisms
E.g., We seek comfort in food or alcohol or project our feelings of shame and blame others for our emotional pain
↓
Undesirable Outcomes
I.e., Suboptimal health, low self-esteem, and unhealthy relationships

Table 2

A Constructive Mindset
I.e., *"One is inherently worthy; External factors, such as one's physical attribute, accomplishment, wealth, material possession, social status, or popularity, does not define an individual."*
↓
Positive Internal Thoughts and Dialogues
I.e., *"I'm inherently worthy; I love myself unconditionally"*
↓
Positive Emotions and Feelings
I.e., Joy, gratitude, hope, and optimism
↓
Healthy Behaviors and Coping Strategies
I.e., We're proactive and engage in responsible self-care
↓
Positive Outcomes
I.e., Optimal health, high self-esteem, and rewarding relationships

Accountability and Empowerment, which is the second book in the series of *The Inner Control Is the True Control*, also directs our focus inwardly to find answers and achieve total wellness.

This book explains that because we have little or no control over the stressors that create emotional distress in our lives, we focus on our own part (i.e., our own ways of thinking, feeling, and behaving) to remain in control and see choices. In other words, *Accountability and Empowerment* encourages us to hold ourselves accountable for our part in our emotional suffering without being self-judgmental or self-critical. This inner control empowers us to retake our personal power, stay focused, achieve our goals, and reach a state of total well-being.

The books in the series of *The Inner Control Is the True Control* were written independently of each other—*Accountability and Empowerment* is not a sequel to *Building a Strong Sense of Self*. Although it is recommended that one reads both books to receive the maximum benefit, readers may choose to read either one independently of the other and still gain a transformative experience.

Control Over Our Inner Thoughts → *Control Over Our Behaviors* → *Control Over Our Life*
(Inner Control) **(True Control)** **(Total Wellness)**

> *We are in control of our lives and destiny when we stay in control of our thoughts and self-talks.*

About This Book

Accountability and Empowerment: A Four-Step Strategy for Overcoming Resentment helps you gain insight and cultivate a conscientious and empowering mindset.

Such a constructive state of mind will empower you to stay focused and in control during times of stress, achieve your goals, and reach your full potential.

To help you build a conscientious and empowering mindset, this book takes you through the process of *genuine accountability*. Working through this unique and effective four-step strategy will change (reframe) the way you perceive unpleasant events or situations.

A true and undistorted perception of reality will change your internal thoughts and self-dialogues and empower you to:
- ◊ Let go of your negative feelings and avoid the physical and mental adverse effects that holding onto such feelings may create in your life;
- ◊ Retake your personal power and see choices and explore all the possibilities; and,
- ◊ Find the path to a state of physical, emotional, and mental well-being.

To demonstrate how the process of genuine accountability can help you develop a conscientious and empowering state of mind and reach total wellness, *Accountability and Empowerment* presents four hypothetical case studies. In all of these scenarios, one is experiencing stress (resentment) in their relationship with someone.

As you work through the steps of the genuine accountability process in each of these case studies, you come to gather and cultivate principles that foster conscientious and empowering internal thoughts and self-dialogues.

Accountability and Empowerment offers positive self-talk scripts at the end of the chapters that are emotionally challenging to work through. These mindfulness scripts will slow down your reading, stimulate critical thinking, reinforce learning, and help you find a sense of calmness and resolve.

The following two workbooks serve as companions to this transformative book:

A Tool for Letting Go of Resentment and Anger: Short. Straightforward. Transformative: This workbook contains self-inquiry questions, worksheets, and inspirational words and quotes to help you let go of your feelings of resentment and prevent their downward spiral.

Like its master book, A *Tool for Letting Go of Resentment and Anger* triggers analytical and critical thinking as it explores the scenarios in which one is experiencing stress (resentment) in their relationship with someone:

I feel offended.
I feel annoyed.
I feel jealous.
I feel that I have been wronged.

The inspirational words and quotes presented in this workbook empower you to regain control, resolve conflicts, and move onward.

A Workbook for Overcoming Resentment: Through offering short and easy-to-read perspectives, this workbook summarizes the root causes of resentment that are explored in *Accountability and Empowerment*—this book is ideal for those who seek answers but prefer reading short books.

Although it is recommended that readers work through all three books to receive the maximum benefit, you can still gain a transformative experience by exploring any of them independently of the others.

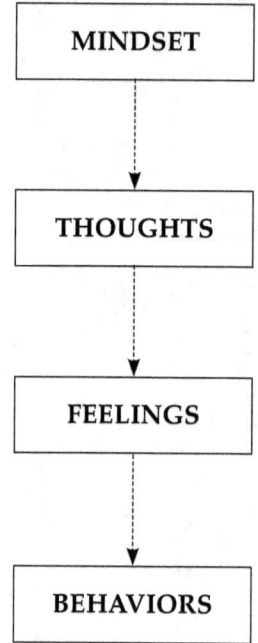

A Note to My Readers

Accountability and Empowerment was written based on the premise that a true transformation and personal growth may not be attained unless we examine the past and make sense of what happened during the early years of our childhood.

This premise is supported by the following understanding:

During the early years of our lives, our brain may save and repress painful memories as well as the negative emotions that are associated with them, such as shame, fear, or guilt.

Our mind hides unpleasant events and emotions from our awareness simply because we are born with only a limited number of primitive coping mechanisms.

In other words, we repress traumatic memories since we are not equipped to protect ourselves from what we, as children, instinctively view as "threats."

Left unresolved, these painful emotions may resurface later in life when they are triggered by a stimulus (i.e., a similar event that generates a perception of threat). In cases like this, we, as adults on autopilot, respond and react to a perception that may not accurately represent the present event.

Revisiting and accessing the painful memories of the past gives us the opportunity to make sense of it all through the lens of an understanding, enlightened, and resilient mindset. This insight is the key to reaching transformation, true emotional healing, and total wellness.

> *Understanding the past empowers us to gain awareness and discover how our unconscious trauma responses harm others and bring us emotional suffering.*

Accountability and Empowerment delivers the knowledge that has been gained through academic and clinical work and the insight that has been acquired through a life's journey in a forthright manner. This approach is based on these beliefs:

1. As mature adults, we are all capable of facing the truth.
2. Insincere communication, such as withholding, sugar-coating, or distorting the truth, not only is unhelpful and disrespectful but may also be damaging.

> *The harsh truth that is expressed from a good place in our heart, rather than a resentful place in our mind, is kind, constructive, and freeing.*

3. Judging and labeling ourselves is harmful: it may limit our potential for change and personal growth. In contrast, making (non-judgmental) observations and labeling our behaviors as are experienced by others (e.g., controlling, aggressive, or victimizing) is transformative: it motivates us to change when we become aware of how our behaviors make other people feel and contribute to our emotional suffering.

4. The key to reaching a state of total wellness is self-awareness: It is only when we are willing to face the harsh truth (i.e., our character flaws) that we get a chance to better ourselves, achieve our full potential, and reach the lasting happiness that we deserve to experience.

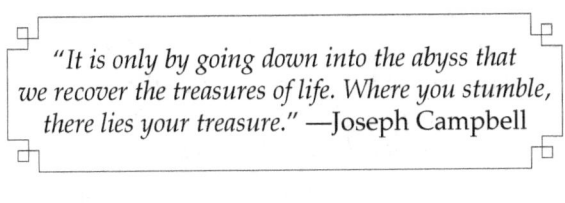

"It is only by going down into the abyss that we recover the treasures of life. Where you stumble, there lies your treasure." —Joseph Campbell

This book defines the term "awakened" as:

A state-of-being in which we are aware of our inner thoughts, feelings, and behaviors. This state of awareness helps us become mindful, make sense of our experience, and see the truth.

When we are mindful, we build a deeper connection with other people since we can better understand their thoughts, feelings, and behaviors and relate to their experiences.

Our mindful and understanding mindset allows us to observe ourselves and others in a non-judgmental manner.

Accountability and Empowerment provokes introspection and raises awareness. Consequently, some painful truths or memories from the past may naturally resurface to the level of conscious awareness and generate inner turmoil, in particular, when you work through Chapters 4 to 7.

For this reason, please read this book with an open mind and forgiving heart towards yourself and those who may have failed you. (Reading the inspirational scripts in *The Inner Control Is the True Control Workbook, Second Edition* is highly recommended for reaching a state of tranquility.)

> *Embark on your journey of self-discovery and never give up—no matter how difficult the path becomes.*
>
> *Keep in mind that suffering is a catalyst for change and personal growth.*

The books in the series of *The Inner Control Is the True Control* were written in response to my clients' request and encouragement. In these books, I have shared not only the information that has helped my clients to achieve a state of physical, emotional, and mental well-being but also the insights that have empowered me (a person who will always be a work-in-progress) to gain clarity, emotional healing, and inner peace.

While writing *Building a Strong Sense of Self* was emotionally difficult—it generated inner turmoil in me as I discovered my own flaws and those of others who had failed me, writing *Accountability and Empowerment* was liberating—it empowered me to retake my personal power and gain a deep sense of inner peace and emotional healing as I found answers and saw my options.

PART I - INTRODUCTION

I started working on *Accountability and Empowerment* in 2016. I finished writing it in 2019 and published the book in 2020.

Writing *Accountability and Empowerment* was instrumental to my transformation and emotional healing.

In the process of completing this book, I came to understand how my unconscious trauma responses that had led me to become complacent in my relationships had caused emotional suffering. Moreover, through the process of brainstorming for this book, I gained a deeper insight into why people, whom I could not relate to, *thought, felt,* or *behaved* the way they did. This understanding mindset and impersonal outlook empowered me to let go of my feelings of resentment, see my options, and move onward and upward.

It is my utmost hope that working through *Accountability and Empowerment* brings you clarity and a sense of empowerment as it has done so for my clients and me.

Before proceeding to Chapter 1, please take some time to reflect and ask yourself the thought-provoking questions that are offered on the next several pages. These questions are designed as such to get you started on the process of introspection.

—A. Sehatti, RN, FNP, MSN

Why is the process of change so difficult?

Among other reasons, changing our habits, behaviors, or lifestyle may be challenging because:

We can only change what we face:
Facing our character flaws and holding ourselves accountable for our mistakes can be a long and painful undertaking. This is especially true for those of us who have used the defense mechanism of avoidance to deal with our setbacks.

Making the right choices is a balancing act:
Finding answers and making right decisions can become confusing and frustrating. This is because the answers don't always lie in our head; Nor do they lie in our heart. They lie deep within us.

Change takes place during the process (this journey is not about the destination):
Staying in the moment, taking small but steady steps, and persevering through adversity is not always easy. Remaining patient and resolute is particularly difficult for those of us who are motivated by immediate gains.

Growth thrives in a favorable environment:
Setting ourselves up for success by creating an environment that is conducive to growth can be challenging. This task is even more difficult to achieve when people in our immediate environment remain unaware and sabotage our growth [because they feel threatened by our transformation].

Making lasting behavioral and lifestyle changes requires determination, great effort, and perseverance.

Source: <u>Building a Strong Sense of Self: Embarking on the Journey of Change</u>

Although the journey of personal growth and transformation is challenging, we go through this life-changing process because we deserve to live a fulfilled life.

Source: <u>The Inner Control Is the True Control Workbook - Second Edition</u>

What Are Some of My Ways of Thinking, Feeling, and Behaving?

1. Do I feel responsible for other people's problems or feelings?
   ☐ Always   ☐ Often   ☐ Occasionally   ☐ Rarely

   If I have answered *Always* or *Often*, then do I help and take care of others even when they are capable of helping themselves (i.e., over-functioning)?
   ☐ Always   ☐ Often   ☐ Occasionally   ☐ Rarely

   If my answer is *Always* or *Often*, then, at the subconscious level, do I over-function for other people because I need to:

   - Be acknowledged that I'm *a good person and worth loving*?
     ☐ Always   ☐ Often   ☐ Occasionally   ☐ Rarely

   - Be affirmed that I'm *good enough, important, or indispensable*?
     ☐ Always   ☐ Often   ☐ Occasionally   ☐ Rarely

   - Be *in control* and *achieve a state of perfection*?
     ☐ Always   ☐ Often   ☐ Occasionally   ☐ Rarely

   If I have answered *Always* or *Often* to any of the above, then do I over-function to such an extent that I become emotionally or physically exhausted?
   ☐ Always   ☐ Often   ☐ Occasionally   ☐ Rarely

   If my answer is *Always* or *Often*, then do I end up feeling unappreciated, used, or taken for granted at some point in time?
   ☐ Always   ☐ Often   ☐ Occasionally   ☐ Rarely

2. When people ask me about my opinions, needs, desires, or

feelings, do I communicate them freely, openly, and without any hesitation?
☐ Always   ☐ Often   ☐ Occasionally   ☐ Rarely

3. Do I feel comfortable saying, "No!" to others?
☐ Always   ☐ Often   ☐ Occasionally   ☐ Rarely

4. Are my own needs, feelings, and thoughts clear to me?
☐ Always   ☐ Often   ☐ Occasionally   ☐ Rarely

5. Does fear of others' angry or retaliatory reactions keep me from expressing myself?
☐ Always   ☐ Often   ☐ Occasionally   ☐ Rarely

6. Does fear of others' judgment, rejection, and abandonment keep me from speaking my truth?
☐ Always   ☐ Often   ☐ Occasionally   ☐ Rarely

7. Do I look to others for reassurance or validation when I need to make decisions?
☐ Always   ☐ Often   ☐ Occasionally   ☐ Rarely

❧ ❧ ❧

8. Do I spend a lot of time thinking about my relationships?
☐ Always   ☐ Often   ☐ Occasionally   ☐ Rarely

9. Do I spend a lot of time thinking about the mistakes that I made during a recent event?
☐ Always   ☐ Often   ☐ Occasionally   ☐ Rarely

10. Do I become self-critical and self-deprecating when I make a mistake?
☐ Always   ☐ Often   ☐ Occasionally   ☐ Rarely

11. Do I feel offended when others point out my mistakes?
☐ Always   ☐ Often   ☐ Occasionally   ☐ Rarely

12. Do I seek other people's feedback and then become offended when I hear their response?
    ☐ Always   ☐ Often   ☐ Occasionally   ☐ Rarely

13. Do I become defensive (i.e., blame, argue excessively, or rationalize to justify my mistakes) when I receive negative feedback?
    ☐ Always   ☐ Often   ☐ Occasionally   ☐ Rarely

14. Do I feel frustrated when others make mistakes?
    ☐ Always   ☐ Often   ☐ Occasionally   ☐ Rarely

15. Do I become annoyed when people deviate from my social norms (i.e., the standards and values that are held by the people in my environment, such as my friends or the society that I live in)?
    ☐ Always   ☐ Often   ☐ Occasionally   ☐ Rarely

16. Do I feel unimportant or insignificant when people don't pay attention to me?
    ☐ Always   ☐ Often   ☐ Occasionally   ☐ Rarely

17. Do I feel unimportant or insignificant when others don't follow my suggestions?
    ☐ Always   ☐ Often   ☐ Occasionally   ☐ Rarely

18. Do others' opposing opinions offend me?
    ☐ Always   ☐ Often   ☐ Occasionally   ☐ Rarely

19. Do I become defensive and argue in an angrily manner when others say something that I strongly disagree with?
    ☐ Always   ☐ Often   ☐ Occasionally   ☐ Rarely

20. Do I need to be right and win arguments to feel that I'm good enough?
    ☐ Always   ☐ Often   ☐ Occasionally   ☐ Rarely

21. Do I need to lead or dominate a conversation to feel that I'm worthy?
    ☐ Always   ☐ Often   ☐ Occasionally   ☐ Rarely

22. Do I compare myself with others and become envious?
    ☐ Always   ☐ Often   ☐ Occasionally   ☐ Rarely

23. When I feel offended, annoyed, or envious, do I externalize my feelings (i.e., take out my frustration on other people)?
    ☐ Always   ☐ Often   ☐ Occasionally   ☐ Rarely

24. Do I blame others when something goes wrong in my life?
    ☐ Always   ☐ Often   ☐ Occasionally   ☐ Rarely

25. When I feel resentful, does my facial expression match my inner feelings?
    ☐ Always   ☐ Often   ☐ Occasionally   ☐ Rarely

26. In my relationships with others, do I address issues as they arise?
    ☐ Always   ☐ Often   ☐ Occasionally   ☐ Rarely

27. When I am hurt or angry, do I use "You" statements to express myself? (E.g., *You are so insensitive!*)
    ☐ Always   ☐ Often   ☐ Occasionally   ☐ Rarely

28. When I'm wronged by others, do I bottle up, withdraw, and see myself as a victim as a way to justify my passivity?
    ☐ Always   ☐ Often   ☐ Occasionally   ☐ Rarely

PART II

Genuine Accountability

1

The Genuine Accountability Process

As we are all aware, we have no or little control over many stressors that create emotional distress in our day-to-day living. However, when we focus on ourselves (i.e., our own part in our emotional experiences), then we become enabled to maintain our personal power and take control of our lives. We can reach this goal by working through the *genuine accountability* process.

This book defines the process of genuine accountability in the following manner:

> *The genuine accountability process is a series of actions taken, while looking inwardly, in order to discover the truth: how our own ways of thinking, feeling, and behaving may play a part in our painful emotional experiences and suffering.*
>
> *In this state of self-awareness, we are able to identify our true feelings; gain insight into our inner thoughts; and, see our patterns of behavioral response to stress through an honest but non-judgmental observation and appraisal of our own self.*

The following four viewpoints aim to demonstrate the importance of self-awareness and self-accountability (genuine accountability) in achieving a state of total wellness.

Perspective 1

During times of stress, we may struggle to stay committed to our healthy behavioral and lifestyle changes and reach such goals as weight loss or long-term sobriety. This may be because our negative emotional experiences trigger a flawed pattern of internal thoughts and dialogues that was programmed in us during the early years of our childhood.

In turn, this conditioned mindset triggers a set of automatic and maladaptive behaviors, such as avoidance coping, to help us deal with our negative feelings. For example, we may drink or eat to gain comfort and avoid experiencing emotional pain.

The following premise may explain why, when we remain unawakened, *one* deviation from our plans could make us lose control, regress to our old behaviors, give up on our goals, and not reach our potential:

> *When we remain unaware, we lose the opportunity to identify our mistakes and remove the obstacles that keep us from attaining our goals.*
>
> *Consequently, we find ourselves facing similar challenges every time we attempt to accomplish a task.*
>
> *As the negative memories associated with each repeated failed attempt become stored in the associative part of our brain, we naturally lose faith in ourselves and our abilities to make significant achievements.*
>
> *This is when we create a downward spiral: we lose motivation and give up on our goals. Others stop believing in us. We experience apathy and feel stuck (Table 3).*

Table 3

We set a goal and come up with a plan of action.
↓
When faced with a difficult situation,
we make a poor choice.
↓
Being on autopilot, this one deviation from our plan
makes us lose control and regress to our old ways
(we experience a relapse).
↓
We lose motivation and fail to reach our goal.

Being on autopilot, we continue to repeat
our maladaptive pattern.
↓
We end up experiencing defeat with
each repeated attempt.
↓
As we lose faith in ourselves, we become
discouraged to try again.
↓
We give up on our goal.
↓
Others lose faith in us.
↓
We experience apathy and feel stuck.

In sum, when we are unaware of our patterns of thoughts, feelings, and behaviors, then we are unable to:
» Gain a true understanding of what is happening during times of stress;
» Face our mistakes and deal with their consequences;
» Learn better ways to cope and deal with setbacks; and,
» Reach our full potential.

On the other hand, when we are awakened, we are aware of our internal thoughts and dialogues that generate our negative feelings and drive our maladaptive responses during times of stress. This state of mindfulness allows us to reach our objectives since we are empowered to make sense of the truth, learn from our mistakes, regain control, and prevent the downward spiral.

We start believing in ourselves when our experiences change. As our positive and rewarding experiences motivate and inspire us to work harder, we create an upward spiral (Table 4).

Table 4

We set a goal and come up with a plan of action.
↓
When faced with a difficult situation, we relapse and make a poor choice.
↓
Being self-aware, we understand what happened and learn from our mistake.
↓
We adjust and commit to our new learnings (e.g., we make a more realistic set of plans).
↓
We reach our goal.

In sum, when we are aware and mindful of our thoughts, feelings, and behaviors, then we are able to:
» Gain a true understanding of what happens during stressful times;
» Hold ourselves accountable for our mistakes and deal with their consequences;
» Learn better ways to cope with challenging situations; and,
» Achieve goals and reach our full potential.

Tables 5 and 6 display and compare two hypothetical case studies in which we set a goal to lose weight and take steps to achieve our target. In the first case study, we are at the automatic state of consciousness and in the second one, we are awakened.

This comparison demonstrates the profound impact our state of mindfulness (an essential component of the process of genuine accountability) has on our ability to face our mistakes and attain our objectives.

Table 5

We make a firm decision to lose weight.
↓
We come up with a plan of action to meet our target.
↓
We experience cravings.
↓
We give in to our temptation and overeat.

Being on autopilot, we view the deviation from our plan through a rigid, perfectionistic, and unrealistic mindset.
↓
We become self-critical and self-blaming (e.g., "*I didn't stick to my plan . . . I was bad; I'll never lose weight . . .*").
↓
We experience feelings of shame, guilt, and anxiety (fear of failure).
↓
We behave automatically.

Our ingrained defense mechanism helps us deal with our negative feelings and regain a sense of inner normalcy. For example, we become self-conciliatory and self-enabling and seek comfort in food while saying to ourselves, "*I'll start my diet tomorrow.*"

Table 6

We make a firm decision to lose weight.
↓
We come up with a plan of action.
↓
We experience cravings.
↓
We give in to our temptation and overeat.

Being self-aware, we view the deviation from our plan through a rational, conscientious, and realistic mindset. Therefore, we form constructive and proactive internal thoughts and dialogues, such as the following:

"I realize that returning to my old patterns of behaviors is a natural aspect of the process of change. Therefore, I will set myself up for success by making such changes as these:
- *» I will set realistic goals (i.e., I will go for excellence and not perfection).*
- *» I will find out what happened and why I relapsed.*
- *» I will hold myself accountable for my behaviors and learn from my mistakes."*

↓

We engage in the process of introspection and self-reflection and find answers. For example, in looking back, we realize that we were unable to control our overeating because we had skipped lunch and therefore we were hungry.

↓

We commit ourselves to new learnings and make new plans. For example, we decide to plan ahead and avoid being hungry by eating three well-balanced meals and healthy snacks. In addition, we set limits with ourselves when we choose or plan to eat a favorite unhealthy food.

↓

We hold ourselves accountable to our new plans.

Perspective 2

When we are awakened, we harbor positive, constructive, and conscientious internal thoughts and self-talks. This mindful and understanding mindset empowers us to look inwardly in a supportive manner to see the truth and resolve problems.

That is to say, when we are in a state of conscious awareness, we face our own flaws in a *non-judgmental* manner; we don't internalize or devalue ourselves as, *"I'm not a good person,"* or that, *"I'm inadequate."* In other words, rather than rejecting ourselves, we take issue with our faulty behaviors and search deep within us to understand the root cause of our mistakes: *"What happened?"* This self-reflection allows us to gain insight into our subconscious thoughts that generate our feelings and drive our mistakes.

As we delve deeper into knowing ourselves on our path to self-discovery, we realize that we learned a set of flawed values, standards, or principles, which have shaped our faulty internal thoughts, during the early years of our childhood. This realization is liberating and empowering since it offers us an opportunity for personal growth: what we have learned, we *can* unlearn.

In sum, through holding ourselves accountable in a non-judgmental manner, we come to discover our maladaptive patterns: we perceive the world through a misguided mindset that triggers negative emotions and brings about our faulty behaviors. This truth sets us free as it gives us a sense of control.

Perspective 3

When we are awakened, our conscientious, constructive, and understanding mindset empowers us to hold others accountable for their wrongdoings towards us in a *supportive* manner as well.

In doing so, we make observations, not judgments. Therefore, we ask people non-critical and constructive questions in order to ascertain the accuracy of our perception and discover the real truth.

It is through this non-judgmental, non-critical, and non-blaming observation of other people's patterns of thoughts, feelings, and behaviors that we become empowered to not to take things personally and remain non-reactive.

Therefore, when we are in a state of conscious awareness, we don't judge and label people who have wronged us as, *"They are not good people,"* or, *"They are inadequate."* Instead, we take issue with their faulty behaviors and ask ourselves such questions as, *"What triggered them to behave the way they did?"*

As we hold others accountable and set healthy personal boundaries in a calm, assertive, and effective manner, we become empowered to resolve issues without compromising our inner peace. This effective way of resolving conflicts in our relationships gives us a sense of liberation and control over our lives.

PART II - CHAPTER ONE

Perspective 4

When we own our feelings and take responsibility for our emotional experiences, we become liberated: we see that we are not stuck and that we can *choose* to change our ways of thinking that drive our maladaptive actions or inactions and result in negative emotional experiences.

In contrast, when we fail to hold ourselves accountable for our emotional suffering, then we may resort to our primal impulses or primitive defense mechanisms to deal with our undesirable feelings and reach a sense of inner normalcy. While many of these conditioned behaviors may bring about a short-term sense of emotional relief, in the long term, they only add to our inner turmoil because they result in negative outcomes.

For example, when we are faced with a setback or adversity, we may knowingly or unknowingly transfer, displace, or project our negative feelings onto others instead of taking responsibility for our experiences. In this case that we divert our attention onto an external source (i.e., other people), we are perceiving and responding to a distorted reality that will result in negative consequences and further emotional pain. Moreover, when we focus on an external source (i.e., other people) that we have no control over, we are not only relinquishing our personal power but also robbing ourselves of the opportunity to change and grow. As our issues remain unresolved, we end up feeling bitter, resentful, and trapped.

Self-Awareness + Self-Accountability = Genuine Accountability

Self-accountability doesn't mean blaming ourselves . . . When we hold ourselves accountable for our part in our conflicts or emotional experiences, we take responsibility for our choices (i.e., our actions or inactions).

Source: <u>A Tool for Letting Go of Resentment and Anger: Short. Straightforward. Transformative.</u>

2

Gaining Control and Reducing Stress Through the Process of Genuine Accountability

When we discover the root cause of our negative feelings and emotional experiences through the process of genuine accountability, then we become empowered to:
- Gain control over our lives;
- Resolve our conflicts and problems;
- Have rewarding relationships with our significant other, friends, co-workers, and others;
- Make healthier lifestyle choices and improve our physical health; and,
- Manage our stress and reach a state of emotional well-being.

Living a life with less stress and more control offers us an enhanced energy of body and mind. Moreover, managing our negative feelings and overcoming emotional experiences, such as resentment, reduces cortisol levels in our blood.

Cortisol is a steroid hormone. It is secreted by the adrenal glands, which are located on top of our kidneys. The hormone cortisol regulates many important functions in our body.

Cortisol is also the primary stress hormone; it is released during times of stress and danger and plays an important role in helping our body respond to such experiences.

Chronic stress leads to prolonged elevation of cortisol levels in our blood. A high level of cortisol over the long term can lead to such health problems as the following:
- Heart disease
- High blood pressure
- Digestive disorders
- Higher blood sugar levels
- Weakened immune system
- Auto-immune disorders
- Psychosomatic symptoms such as dizziness, muscle aches, or backaches
- Mental health problems such as depression and anxiety

Therefore, gaining control and managing our stress is important in improving our physical, mental, and emotional health and reaching total wellness.

3

The Four-Steps of the Genuine Accountability Process

This book establishes four steps in the process of genuine accountability. Working through this four-step strategy enables us to discover our part in our emotional suffering and regain our control during times of stress. These steps are as follows:

Step 1: While staying in the moment, we connect with our inner self and become aware of the emotions that we are feeling.

Without being judgmental towards ourselves, we make a list of our negative feelings—we understand that *all* of the emotions that one feels is a part of the human experience. Hence, our feelings are all real, valid, and acceptable.

Just as our experiences belong to us, so do our emotions. Hence, we own our negative feelings and take responsibility for managing them.

Step 2: While remaining supportive towards ourselves, we reflect on the stressful event. Since we seldom have control over the stressor, we focus on ourselves to see the truth and understand what happened. By working through this step,

A. We uncover our internal thoughts and dialogues that generate our painful feelings;

B. We become mindful of the deep-seated emotions that trigger our perception (our internal thoughts); and,

C. We discover the root cause of our emotional experience (the reason we feel the way we do).

This second step of the genuine accountability process is based on the following premise:

The deep-seated emotions associated with the repressed memories from the past, along with the values and principles that we have learned in the early years of our childhood shape the way we view the world around us later in life. It is this perception that impacts our internal thoughts and self-talks; and, it is this mindset that generates our feelings and drives our behaviors when we live on autopilot.

Step 3: While we continue to engage in introspection and self-reflection, we discover our part in our emotional suffering:

A. We become aware of our automatic response to stress (our conditioned defense mechanism) that results in negative consequences and leads to emotional pain; and,

B. We gain knowledge and find out how we developed our flawed patterns of coping. It has to be noted that many experts believe:

We learn our ways of coping with our painful emotions during the early years of our childhood as we interact with our immediate environment (i.e., parents). As children, this learned pattern of thinking, feeling, and behaving helps us to distort our reality and regain a sense of control and inner normalcy that is lost during painful or traumatic experiences.

Our defense mechanisms become conditioned in us when we continue using them to deal with our unpleasant feelings and emotional experiences as we are growing older and transitioning into adulthood.

While these primitive coping strategies helped us feel safe during the early years of childhood, they become maladaptive and damaging later in life because they result in negative consequences.

Step 4: Having discovered our part in our emotional suffering, we become enabled to maintain our personal power and regain our control in our lives. Since we *can* stay calm and non-reactive, we *can*:

A. See choices and consider all of our options;
B. Make well-thought-out decisions that are based on free will, sound principles, logical reasonings, and virtues of love and humanity;
C. Resolve issues;
D. Learn from our mistakes and make constructive changes;
E. Develop healthy coping strategies; and,
F. Commit to new learnings.

In summary, we undergo the four steps of the process of genuine accountability to deal with our unpleasant feelings and emotional experiences. As we work through each step of the process, we come to gather information about ourselves and gain insight into our patterns of feeling, thinking, and behaving. We come to our knowledge through observation, introspection, and inquiry (asking ourselves thought-provoking questions). By processing the information and making sense of it all—the Aha Moment—we come to identify and take responsibility for our own part in our emotional suffering. Holding ourselves accountable empowers us to maintain our personal power and stay in control of the choices we make in our lives. As we resolve our problems, we transform and reach a state of equanimity. Table 7 summarizes the steps of the genuine accountability process.

Table 7

The Four Steps of the Genuine Accountability Process

Step 1

We identify, acknowledge, and own our negative feelings in a non-judgmental manner.

Step 2

We understand what happened and discover the root cause of our emotional experience:
 a. We uncover our deep seated emotions and inner thoughts that generate our painful feelings; and,
 b. We gain insight into ourselves and become aware of the values and principles that have shaped our inner thoughts and self-talks (our mindset).

Step 3

We identify our part in our emotional suffering:
 a. We discover our own faulty behaviors (our reaction to the stressor) and face their negative consequences; and,
 b. We find out how we developed our general patterns of coping with painful emotions and feelings.

Step 4

We effectively deal with our negative feelings, resolve issues, learn from our mistakes, make constructive changes (develop healthy and effective coping strategies), commit to our new learnings, and reach a state of inner calmness.

In order to demonstrate how working through the process of genuine accountability empowers us to reach our full potential and achieve total wellness, we look at a hypothetical case study in which we are experiencing displeasure in our relationship with someone. This negative emotional experience will hereafter be referred to as *resentment*.

As we work through the first step of the process of genuine accountability to deal with our resentment, we connect with our inner self and identify our feelings by asking ourselves such questions as (Table 8):

» *Why am I experiencing resentment?*
» *What is happening?*
» *'What' do I feel?*
» *Do I feel offended?*
» *Do I feel annoyed?*
» *Do I feel jealous? Or,*
» *Do I feel that I have been wronged?*

Table 8

Why am I experiencing resentment?
What is happening? 'What' do I feel?

Do I feel offended?	*Do I feel annoyed?*	*Do I feel jealous?*	*Do I feel that I have been wronged?*

The next four chapters explore the following situations and demonstrate how working through the steps of the genuine accountability process empowers us to overcome resentment:

» *I'm experiencing resentment because I feel offended.*
(Chapter 4)
» *I'm experiencing resentment because I feel annoyed.*
(Chapter 5)
» *I'm experiencing resentment because I feel jealous.*
(Chapter 6)
» *I'm experiencing resentment because I feel that I have been wronged.*
(Chapter 7)

PART II - CHAPTER THREE

> *Just like working out strengthens our muscles; helps us build endurance; and, enables us to do things that we weren't able to do before, working through the process of genuine accountability strengths the executive part of our brain (i.e., neuroplasticity); helps us build emotional stamina; and, enables us to deal with challenging interactions the way we weren't able to do before.*
>
> Source: <u>A Tool for Letting Go of Resentment and Anger: Short. Straightforward. Transformative.</u>

THE GENUINE ACCOUNTABILITY PROCESS
A Four-Step Strategy for Dealing With Our Negative Emotions in Times of Stress

STEP 1	STEP 2	STEP 3	STEP 4
Feelings: We own our emotional experience	*Thoughts:* We become aware of our deep thoughts and discover the root cause of our *emotional experience*	*Behaviors:* We see our part in our *emotional suffering* (i.e., our actions or inactions)	*Response:* We explore our choices and take appropriate action(s)

> *Retake your personal power.*
> *Our emotional experience doesn't have to result in emotional suffering.*

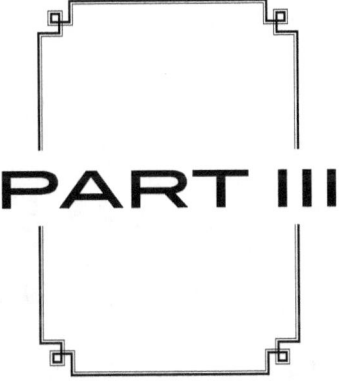

PART III

Overcoming Resentment Through the
Process of Genuine Accountability

*Letting go of our feelings of resentment does not
mean accepting other people's hurtful behaviors;
Nor does it mean blaming ourselves for our feelings of
hurt, anger, frustration, disgust, hatred, or jealousy . . .*

*Rather, letting go of our feelings of resentment
is about genuinely releasing such feelings
so that we could emotionally detach ourselves
from those whom we resent:*

*For it is when we are emotionally free that
we can think clearly, see our choices, and
lead a proactive and fulfilling life.*

*Then, in essence, to let go of our feelings
of resentment is to retake our personal power
and control over our lives.*

*Let your feelings of resentment awaken and
mobilize you, not enslave you.*

*Source: <u>A Tool for Letting Go of Resentment and Anger:
Short. Straightforward. Transformative.</u>*

4

I Feel Offended

This chapter explores a hypothetical case study in which we are experiencing resentment towards other people because we are feeling offended by their behavior. These are some examples of such a situation:

» We receive negative feedback. For example, our boss makes an issue over our tardiness or lack of commitment to make a deadline.

» People don't make an exception for us, give us preferential treatment, or pay us the attention we expect to receive. For instance, a receptionist doesn't bend the rules for us.

» We don't receive a response that we had hoped for or expected. For example, we ask a friend for her opinion on how we look and she says, "What you are wearing doesn't look good on you."

» People give us solicited advice that we find unpleasant or offensive to hear. For example, our doctor says that we are overweight and need to lose weight or that we should stop drinking because our liver enzymes are elevated.

This chapter demonstrates how working through the process of genuine accountability helps us reach a state of equanimity by focusing on one of the above scenarios: *I feel offended because I have received negative feedback from someone.*

I Feel Offended Because I Have Received Negative Feedback From Someone (Referred to as 'Person A')

Step 1

As the first step in the process of genuine accountability, we list the feelings that Person A's remark has generated in us.

We own and validate all of the negative emotions that we can feel (e.g., insulted, hurt, angry, enraged, and/or hatred) while keeping in mind that:

- As humans, we feel a wide range of emotions.
- All of our emotions are real, valid, and acceptable.
- Our negative feelings become dysfunctional when we act upon them and become reactive (e.g., when we make an unkind comment to deliberately inflict pain because we are feeling offended).

These understandings allow us to validate our feelings in a non-judgmental manner. Since we have no control over Person A's thoughts, feelings, or behaviors, acknowledging and owning those of our own, without judging ourselves, becomes the key to maintaining control and managing our emotional state.

Step 2

In the second step of the process of genuine accountability, we connect with our inner self and become self-reflective. The knowledge that we gain through this step of the process helps us: 1) Become aware of our deep thoughts and self-talks that have generated our negative feelings (i.e., listed in Step 1); and, 2) Discover the root cause of our emotional experience.

The following thought-provoking questions demonstrate how we achieve these objectives through the process of self-inquiry:

◊ Why does Person A's comment make me feel offended?

◊ What are my thoughts? Do I believe that Person A's feedback is inaccurate? If yes, then do I think that Person A has meant to hurt my feelings?
  - If yes, then is this an assumption or have I checked my reality and asked for a clarification? (Refer to Chapter 7 if you believe that someone has meant to offend you).
  - If no, then why do I feel offended? Do I believe that the comment has not captured the truth because Person A has formed a wrong opinion of me? In other words, do I feel offended and resentful because I believe that Person A has judged me? If yes, then what has stopped me from resolving the issue (perhaps a misunderstanding) by expressing myself in an effective and non-reactive manner?

◊ Or, deep down, do I believe that Person A's feedback is accurate? If yes, then why do I feel offended?
  - Could it be because I think that the comment was delivered in a critical and belittling manner? If yes, then what do I think was happening? Have I asked what provoked Person A to express themselves in such a disrespectful way? Have I tried to resolve the issue by expressing myself and setting healthy boundaries in a non-reactive and non-provocative manner (e.g., *"Although I appreciate your helpful feedback, I take issue with the way it was conveyed to me"*)?
  - However, if the feedback is *accurate* and *constructive* and was delivered *respectfully*, then why do I feel the way I do? Is it possible that, at the subconscious level, Person A's remark has:

» Touched an inner wound in me (i.e., triggered a painful memory from the past);
» Evoked such deep-seated emotions as shame ("*I'm not good enough*"), guilt ("*I'm bad*"), or fear ("*I'll be judged, rejected, and abandoned*");
» Elicited a perception of threat to the sense of identity that I developed in the early years of my childhood ("*I'm special . . . better . . . or superior to others; I need to be perfect to be enough . . .*");
» Triggered my defense mechanisms (i.e., *projection*); and,
» Generated such *defensive* inner thoughts and self-talks as: "*I'm being attacked, judged, belittled, or stripped of my identity?*"

If so, then could this be why I'm feeling offended now? If yes, then is it fair to conclude that my feelings of resentment have been generated by a distorted *perception* of reality?

※ ※ ※

Now that we have gained a better understanding into what has happened, we dig deeper within to discover the root cause of our emotional experience by asking ourselves such questions as these:

◊ Do I generally perceive a sense of threat to my self-value or self-importance when I receive negative feedback? To put it differently, does facing my mistakes or wrongdoings (i.e., my humanness) trigger feelings of shame and inadequacy in me? If yes, then why? Could it be because I expect myself to be perfect?

◊ In general, do I need to be affirmed or acknowledged by other people to think that I'm good enough? Do I need to receive reassurance or praise to think that I'm adequate? If yes, then why? Why do I need to be affirmed or praised by other people to think well of myself? Why am I needy of others' approval to experience a sense of inner normalcy?

◊ Could it be because I define my value or worth as a person based on such external factors as *perfection* or *what others think of me*? If yes, then how was my brain programmed to harbor such thoughts or values? I know that I was not born with my character traits (i.e., ways of thinking, feeling, and behaving), so how did I learn to think the way I do now?

As mentioned earlier, many psychologists believe that we learn our ways of thinking during the early years of our childhood as we interact with our parents or parent figures. These values, beliefs, and standards become reinforced and conditioned in us by the environment we grow up in. For more information on this subject, refer to *Building a Strong Sense of Self: Embarking on the Journey of Change*.

Step 3

In this step of the process of genuine accountability, we observe ourselves in a non-judgmental manner and become aware of our patterns of behavioral response to stress (our defense mechanism).

In the same way, we observe others in a non-judgmental and non-reactive manner and gain an understanding of how our coping strategies are making them feel and respond to us.

The insight that we gain through these observations allows us to discover our own part in our emotional suffering.

Holding ourselves accountable empowers us to be in control of our emotional experience. Keeping our personal power and being in control of our lives is paramount to reaching total wellness and inner peace.

Through engaging in deep reflection, this step also helps us gain an insight into how we developed our general patterns of coping with stress. This knowledge gives us the opportunity to differentiate, grow, and learn better ways to deal with challenging situations and resolve our unpleasant feelings.

The following self-inquiry questions demonstrate how we can achieve these stated objectives:

◊ In general, how do I deal with my painful emotions (i.e., shame, anxiety, or anger) when I feel offended? Do these emotions trigger a conditioned pattern of behaviors in me? In other words, when I feel offended, do I become reactive and behave automatically to reach a sense of inner normalcy? For example, do I:
  » Ridicule or tease?
  » Use sarcasm?
  » Badmouth or make disparaging remarks about the person whose action I perceive as offensive?
  » Engage in power-struggles or defiance?
  » Become rebellious?
  » Withdraw love (e.g., give the cold shoulder)?
  » Use physical force against the person whose actions I perceive as belittling and insulting?

◊ If yes to any of the above, then how do I think my defensive behaviors would make other people feel? How do I expect them to respond to my reactivity?

- If others also become reactive and respond to me in a harmful manner, then do I see their action (their defense mechanism) as a rejection of my behaviors? Or, do I take it personally and perceive their response as a rejection of *Me*, as a person?

- If I feel rejected or victimized by other people's response, then how do I deal with my painful emotions? Do I acknowledge and take responsibility for my wrongdoings (*resilience*) or do I use such strategies as *avoidance* (e.g., seeking comfort in food or alcohol), *resistance* (e.g., rationalizing, justifying, or arguing), or *projection* (e.g., blaming) to cope and gain a sense of inner normalcy?

- Do my ways of coping during such stressful times result in positive emotional and social outcomes or do they produce inner turmoil, emotional suffering, and social isolation?

- How did I learn my coping strategies?

- When I was a young child, how did my parents or parent figures regain their control during times of stress? What was their predominant defense mechanism?

The experts believe that we learn our ways of behaving, defending ourselves, and coping with stressful situations as we interact with our immediate environment in the early years of our childhood. (Refer to *Building a Strong Sense of Self: Embarking on the Journey of Change* for more information on this subject.)

Having gained insight into our patterns of thinking, feeling, and behaving, we may now have a better understanding as to what happened, why we feel offended, and how our own character flaws (i.e., maladaptive ways of thinking and coping), which we learned in the early years of our childhood, could lead to negative outcomes and emotional suffering (Table 9).

Understanding the truth and holding ourselves accountable liberates us and empowers us to see that we are not trapped: We have a choice; *We can change our part to change the dynamics of our relationships or interactions with others.*

This awareness takes us to Step 4 of the process of genuine accountability.

Step 4

Working through this final step of the genuine accountability process empowers us to deal with our feelings of resentment, resolve issues, and make constructive changes (i.e., turn our negative ways of thinking and automatic ways of behaving into constructive self-talks and well-thought-out coping strategies).

Through continue exploring the hypothetical case study, *I feel offended because I received a negative feedback from Person A*, the following internal contemplations demonstrates how we can achieve these objectives and reach a state of equanimity:

◊ Having discovered the root cause of my resentment, I am now empowered to see choices. This sense of control enables me to remain non-reactive and consider such options as:

A. *Avoid* the source of stress: Cut off or distance myself from Person A;

B. *Accept*: Acknowledge my own humanness and see my *Total Self* (*my strengths, weaknesses, and limitations*), let go of my feelings of resentment, and thank Person A for their constructive feedback; and/or,

Table 9

I Feel Offended

In the early years of our childhood, we may develop a false sense of self-identity when we receive a lot of praise, recognition, or reward for such factors as our physical attributes, intelligence, talents, or behaviors.

This is because, in such situations, we learn to measure our value or worth, as a person, based on how others think of us: *"I'm special . . . I'm better . . . I'm prettier . . . I'm more intelligent . . . I'm superior to my siblings; I should always be perfect, better, or superior to others in order to be adequate."*

When we remain unaware and transition into adulthood with such a mindset, we come to face many challenges and negative experiences. For example, we may become overly self-judgmental and self-critical when we deviate from our own unrealistically high standards: *"I'm inadequate because I made a mistake."*

Maintaining healthy relationships is another challenge that we may face as adults. For example, in our relationships with others, we may take things personally when:

» We receive negative feedback instead of getting praise or affirmation: *"I'm being judged; I'm inadequate."*
» We don't receive the attention or favorable treatment that we think we deserve: *"I'm not worthy or important enough."*

At the subconscious level, such internal thoughts and self-talks generate emotions of shame (*"I'm not good enough"*), fear and anxiety (*"I'll be rejected and abandoned"*), and anger (*"I'm being insulted"*): We become resentful.

Being on autopilot, these unpleasant emotions and feelings trigger our conditioned defense mechanism: We become defensive.

Our automatic response, which insulates us against experiencing inner unrest during our childhood, not only doesn't help us later in life but also leads to undesirable outcomes (e.g., dysfunctional relationships).

Over time, our accumulated negative experiences may erode our self-esteem and lead to a state of despair, apathy, and unhappiness.

C. *Change* my character flaws (i.e., *my weaknesses*): Cultivate a set of sound principles that generate constructive and healthy ways of thinking, feeling, and behaving.

◊ After thinking things through and considering the possible outcomes and consequences associated with each of the options, I will arrive at the following conclusions:
  » While avoidance may offer emotional relief in the short term, it may not be the best choice in the long run since it will not resolve my issue.
  » Furthermore, cutting off or distancing myself from others (when unwarranted) may deprive me of rewarding experiences and opportunities.
  » Therefore, I will choose the combination of the options B and C. Thus, I will:
    • Accept my humanness (i.e., my imperfections);
    • Overcome my feelings of resentment and express my gratitude; and,
    • Better myself by adopting sound principles, values, and standards that foster healthier attitudes towards myself and others.

◊ When I cultivate a constructive mindset that is founded on sound principles, then my perceptions, thoughts, and self-dialogues would change. A positive outlook will generate positive feelings and drive a set of healthy behaviors and coping strategies. For example, when I don't allow external factors, such as perfection or what others think of me, to define me, then my internal thoughts and dialogues would be like these:

It is my responsibility to acknowledge and affirm my Self; I don't need to be affirmed or acknowledged by others to know that I'm good enough. I don't need to fix others, be right, or win arguments to know that I'm important or good enough. I am good enough; I am inherently worthy.

I am an imperfect human being; My flaws are part of my humanness. Making mistakes is a natural part of the human experience.

Now, I will see my mistakes as an opportunity for growth and change. I will consider other people's feedback, suggestions, or advice with an open mind. Therefore,

» *I will define one's reality as the person's truth that is gained through observation. Accordingly, I will see others' constructive feedback as their reality that is being openly and candidly offered to me.*

» *I will see people's well-intentioned suggestions or advice as their opinion, insight, or knowledge that is kindly shared with me.*

» *These healthy and positive internal thoughts and dialogues will empower me to overcome my feelings of resentment and stay non-judgmental, receptive, tolerant, and serene.*

» *Being in a state of harmony and equanimity, as opposed to being in a state of hostility and enmity, will allow me to remain non-reactive when I'm faced with challenging situations. Since the prefrontal cortex (thinking brain) will be more available to me in such a state of mind, I will be empowered to regulate my impulses and become a more reflective observer and learner.*

In summary, when we face and accept our humanness and change our faulty ways of thinking (our mindset) by adopting constructive principles, we will become empowered to remain secure and confident in our relationships and experience a state of equanimity and inner harmony. This state of being will lead to rewarding outcomes and a sense of total wellness.

A Mindfulness Script

> *Please pause a moment, take a few slow and deep breaths, and then read this script aloud.*

During the very early years of my childhood, I looked at my parent(s) and saw myself through their eyes as someone who was special, flawless, and worthy of praise and attention.

Naturally, I grew up expecting to find the same image in everyone's eyes. I felt hurt and offended when I saw my flaws, imperfections, and humanness instead.

Unable to face the truth, I numbed my emotional pain and distorted my reality: *"I'm deserving of receiving high praise, attention, and unconditional love from everyone; I'm being judged and victimized by those who give me a negative feedback, hold me accountable, set limits for me, or don't affirm or acknowledge me."*

Over time, the accumulated resentments turned into grievances. As I couldn't see the truth, I found myself feeling stuck; Naturally, I wallowed in self-pity: *"Poor me!"* This was when I stopped believing in myself.

Having gained an understanding mindset, I now hold myself accountable for my part in my emotional suffering.

My self-discovery humbles me.

Acknowledging and accepting my humanness liberates me: it allows me to forgive myself for not knowing any better.

Accountability and Empowerment

> *Please pause a moment and take a few slow and deep breaths before continuing to read this script aloud.*

Having gained more knowledge on my path to personal growth, I'm now empowered to see that, as a mature adult, it is my responsibility to acknowledge and affirm myself.

Now, I'm aware that:
My mistakes or flaws don't define me;
I am good enough;
I matter; and,
I am worthy.

Now that I love myself unconditionally, I don't need attention from others to know that I'm good enough.

Now, my internal thoughts and self-talks are no longer like this:

"I should think, feel, or behave in a certain way so that everyone would like me, approve of me, or regard me as adequate or worthy."

Now, when I receive well-intentioned feedback from other people, I embrace it and see it as an opportunity for self-improvement. Thus, I will listen and consider it with an open mind and a grateful heart.

Now, I don't become resentful when I'm held accountable for my mistakes.

Now, I know that people's rejection of my behavior is not a rejection of me or a measure of my value or worth as a person.

This positive mindset empowers me to manage my emotions, gain control over my behaviors, reach my full potential, and live a fulfilled life.

> *Please stay in the present moment!*

> *"You're unique but you're NOT special."*
> *Does this premise make you feel liberated?*
> *Or, does it make you feel offended?*

> *In natural and healthy relationships,*
> *people feel free to speak directly, openly, truthfully,*
> *and in a non-premeditated manner.*
>
> *In such relationships, would one feel free to offer*
> *unsolicited feedback or advice?*

> *Criticizing ≠ Offering Feedback*
> *Lecturing ≠ Giving Advice*

> We may not be receptive to honest feedback, advice, or suggestions from others, when we harbor such internal thoughts and self-talks as:
>
> *"I need to be all knowing, perfect, and better than others to be good enough.*
> *When people point out my mistakes, give me advice, or suggest that I do something, then that means that they perceive me as inadequate and less than them."*

> *Natural, rewarding, and healthy human interactions take place in relationships where all parties are willing to receive constructive feedback or advice that is offered respectfully.*

Part III - Chapter Four

> *Are one's ego and the vulnerable inner core the two sides of the same coin?*

> *When one's ego defends a vulnerable inner core then they may need to set rigid boundaries to protect their 'Self.'*

> *When we don't have a positive self-image, we constantly worry about what other people think of us.*
>
> *When we remain unaware and live on autopilot, our fears of others' judgment, rejection, and abandonment, inadvertently, drive our defensive behaviors and result in people judging, rejecting, and abandoning us.*
>
> *The problem gets even worse when we judge, reject, and abandon those who attempt to share constructive feedback with us.*
>
> *This is how we get stuck in a downward spiral of anxiety and depression.*
>
> *Believe in yourself;*
> *Build a strong sense of your Self.*
>
> *Source: <u>A Tool for Letting Go of Resentment and Anger: Short. Straightforward. Transformative</u>.*

> *Build a strong sense of your Self and make a safe environment for others to express themselves and be true to you—because, you deserve nothing less.*

> *You deserve to live a fulfilled life. So, ask people you trust for their honest feedback; practice self-reflection; and, become self-aware.*

> When we gain awareness and reach a genuine state of equanimity, we gratefully remember those who shared a harsh truth, held us accountable, or refused to make an exception for us.
>
> They helped us become aware of our character flaws, take responsibility for our mistakes, and keep our expectations in check.
>
> In short, they empowered us to grow and reach our full potential.

Part III - Chapter Four

Now that I see my part in my emotional suffering, what are my choices?

How can I regain my inner peace?

> *Turn your flaws into your strengths:*
> *Change your negative ways of thinking and automatic*
> *ways of behaving into constructive self-talks and*
> *well-thought-out coping strategies.*

5
I Feel Annoyed

This chapter explores a hypothetical case study in which we are experiencing resentment towards others because we are annoyed by their ways of thinking, feeling, or behaving (character traits), even though our rights are not being violated by them. Some examples of such a situation would be when people:
- » Seek attention, affirmation, or acknowledgment
- » Display emotions openly
- » Become overly attentive to us
- » Ask us questions
- » Make mistakes
- » Appear self-assured or speak confidently
- » Disagree with our opinion or hold a certain view or belief that is different from ours
- » Speak directly and straightforwardly of a harsh truth that is difficult for us to hear

This chapter demonstrates how by working through the genuine accountability process we become empowered to deal with our feelings of annoyance without compromising our relationships.

To better understand this process, the next sections will focus on one of the above situations by using this scenario: *I feel annoyed when my co-worker makes a mistake.*

I Feel Annoyed When My Co-Worker (Referred to as 'Person B') Makes a Mistake

Step 1

In the first step of the process of genuine accountability, we identify and list the feelings that such a situation generates in us (e.g., irritation, frustration, contempt, disgust, anger, and/or rage). Since we have no control over Person B's way of thinking, feeling, or behaving, owning and acknowledging our negative feelings in a non-judgmental manner allows us to keep our personal power and take control of our own behaviors and emotional state.

Step 2

In the second step of the genuine accountability process, we connect with our inner self and gain insight into our internal thoughts, self-talks, and deep-seated emotions that are evoked by the present event.

The knowledge that we gather through this step of the process enables us to: 1) Become aware of the deep thoughts and self-talks that have generated our negative feelings (i.e., listed in Step 1); and, 2) Discover the root cause of our emotional experience.

We reach these objectives by asking ourselves such thought-provoking questions as the following:

◊ Why do I feel annoyed? Why does Person B's mistake annoy me if it doesn't violate my rights or the rights of others who need to be defended?

◊ Do I feel frustrated because Person B doesn't do things the way I think they *should*? In other words, do I have a problem with Person B's performance because it doesn't meet my standards?

◊ If yes, then what internal thoughts and emotions does this *deviation from my standards* generate in me? Deep down, do I think that Person B is incompetent or incapable (*"Person B is inadequate"*)? Do I think that I'm better than Person B (*"Person B is less than me because I wouldn't make such a mistake"*)?

◊ If yes, then what makes me to form such *an opinion* of Person B? In other words, why do I define and evaluate Person B based on their flawed performance? Do I generally expect people to act flawlessly to consider them *adequate*?

◊ If I evaluate people and measure their performance based on such unrealistic expectations, then do I equally hold myself accountable to the same standards?

◊ If I hold myself accountable to such high standards as well, then why do I neglect to see my humanness? Why do I expect myself or others to be perfect to be good enough? How was my brain programmed to harbor such an all-or-nothing mindset? How did I learn to become a perfectionist?

◊ Moreover, if I search deep within, do I find myself having an urge to fix Person B? Do I think that it's *my responsibility* to do so (*"I should fix others"*)? If yes, then why? Is it possible that I have a *need* to control my environment (i.e., Person B) to gain a sense of inner normalcy? If yes, then why is that?

◊ I know that I was not born with my values or ways of thinking, then how did I develop such a state of mind?

◊ When I was growing up, was I assigned with the parental role? For example, did I assume responsibility for my siblings (or my parents) because I was viewed as being more capable than others in my family? Was I allowed or encouraged (or even expected of) to take over and make decisions that ordinarily a parent would make?

◊ If yes, did I receive attention, recognition, or praise for this over-functioning?

◊ If yes, then did I grow up learning that my value or worth as a person was defined by my performance (i.e., the level of my competence, achievements, or accomplishments or fixing and taking care of others)?

◊ If, as a child, striving for flawlessness made me feel worthy, secure, and in control, then did a deviation from perfection generate feelings of anxiety in me? In other words, did I perceive myself as being inadequate when I made mistakes? Did I worry about what other people thought of me? Did I fear others' judgment, rejection, and abandonment?

◊ Moreover, did I become anxious and irritable when the performance of the people around me (i.e., my siblings or parents) deviated from perfection? Did I develop an urge to cross their boundaries and fix them? If yes, then was I allowed, enabled, or even encouraged to do so? If yes, then did I perceive those people as being less than me or my subordinates?

◊ If yes, then is it possible that, at the subconscious level, Person B's mistake (*a deviation from perfection*) triggers the memories from the past and makes me become anxious, look down on Person B, and control the situation (e.g., fix Person B's mistake)?

◊ In other words, could it be that I feel annoyed because I'm redirecting my own feelings of anxiety towards Person B (or others who make mistakes)?

Or,

◊ Does Person B's mistake annoy me because it deviates from my social norm—the standards and values held by the group of people that I associate with, such as my circle of friends or the society that I live in? In other words, could it be that I feel frustrated because Person B doesn't act in a manner in which I deem appropriate or *proper*?

◊ If yes, then what internal thoughts and deep-seated emotions does this *deviation from my norm*—the way one *should* think, feel, or behave—generate in me?

◊ Do I perceive Person B as inadequate? Deep down, do I think that they are beneath me?

◊ If yes, then, at the subconscious level, does this perception trigger a sense of threat to my self-value when I am around Person B? Does it evoke such deep-seated emotions and feelings as shame (*"I'm embarrassed for Person B"*) and anxiety (*"I feel embarrassed to be connected with Person B; I fear people's judgment, rejection, and abandonment if I'm seen with Person B"*)?

◊ If so, then in such a case as this, could it be that I'm redirecting my own feelings of anxiety towards Person B? Could this be why I feel annoyed now?

◊ If yes, then do I generally tend to define my value as a person or evaluate other people's worth based on what others think?

◊ If yes, then, in general, do I need to fit in or be accepted by people in my social circle to feel that I'm good enough? Moreover, do I tend to form opinions or make choices that are based on "what other people think" rather than "what I believe" is right?

◊ If yes, then why? I know that I was not born with my values or ways of thinking, so how did I develop such a mindset? Was I raised by parents or parent figures who evaluated themselves or others based on external factors, such as what other people thought of them? (Refer to *Building a Strong Sense of Self: Embarking on the Journey of Change* for more discussions on this subject.)

Or,

◊ Do I feel annoyed because Person B's mistake has disrupted my routine or ritual norm (a set of activities or habits that we carry out unconsciously or consciously in order to control or stop our feelings of anxiety or ruminative thinking)?

◊ If so, then do I generally maintain *rigid* routines or rituals in my life? If yes, then do I feel irritable or anxious when there is a deviation in these routines or rituals? Moreover, do I feel uneasy when there is a lack of structure or order in my environment? If yes, then why?

◊ Could it be because, at the subconscious level, such a situation triggers a perception of threat to my sense of inner security? If so, then could this distorted perception evoke my deep-seated fears (i.e., fears of the unknown, uncertainty, and loss of control), generate the feelings of anxiety, and create an intense urge to control my environment?

◊ In other words, is it possible that I automatically and unconsciously control my environment so that I could maintain order and gain a sense of inner security, safety, and normalcy?

◊ If yes, then, at the conscious level, could this urge or deep desire for control generate such thoughts as, *"Person B is incompetent . . . I'd be better off if I do things myself?"*

◊ If yes, then do such internal dialogues generate feelings of frustration? If yes, then could this be why I am feeling annoyed now and have an urge to over-function (or control Person B)?

◊ In other words, could it be that I feel annoyed because I'm redirecting my own feelings of anxiety towards Person B?

◊ If yes, then how did I develop such a mindset? I know that I was not born with it.

◊ Did I grow up in a conflict-laden or chaotic household during the early years of my childhood?

◊ Was I raised by parents or parent figures, such as older siblings, who took their stress out on me because they had poor emotion regulation abilities?

◊ During the early years of my childhood, was I shamed, emotionally degraded, or humiliated (i.e., ridiculed, yelled at, or physically disciplined) during mishaps (i.e., when I made a mistake and was told that I wasn't a *"good child"*)? Was I guilted into conformity? Was I sexually abused?

◊ If I responded YES to all or any of the above questions, then was I defended or protected by any of my parents or parent figures during those traumatic times?

◊ If I was not protected or defended as a child, then how did I deal with such emotions of fear and anxiety? Did I learn to use such defense strategies as the following to cope and regain a sense of safety and inner normalcy:

» Established and maintained a daily routine or set of rituals?
» Over-functioned and took on the parental role (e.g., took responsibility for creating peace in my family, attended to the feelings of others, or solved other people's problems)?
» Broke free from reality through such measures as:
  • Mental escape (e.g., maintained intense concentration on a task to achieve perfect order, symmetry, neatness, or precision)?
  • Physical escape (e.g., found a secret hiding place to play)?

◊ If yes, then did any of these coping mechanisms result in rewarding outcomes? For instance, when I was a child, did I receive recognition or praise for fixing, making peace, or taking care of others (i.e., my siblings)?

◊ If yes, then did I develop a distorted self-identity (i.e., low self-worth) and falsely learned that I was worthy and safe when I helped, fixed, and over-functioned? If yes, then could this be why I *need* to take over when others make mistakes?

◊ Moreover, if consistency (sticking to what was familiar) made me feel safe and secure during childhood, then did a deviation from this state generate anxiety in me? If yes, then could this be why I now have a problem with those behaviors of others that result in a deviation from the standards that are *familiar* to me?

Step 3

In the third step of the process of genuine accountability, we focus on our automatic behaviors (our defense mechanism) that are triggered by our negative feelings and inner thoughts.

While observing ourselves in a non-judgmental manner, we become aware of our patterns of behavioral response to our feelings of annoyance.

In the same manner, we observe other people (i.e., Person B) in a non-judgmental and calm way and understand how our behaviors make them feel and respond to us.

The insight that we gain through our observations allows us to discover our part in our emotional suffering. When we hold ourselves accountable for our part in our unhappiness, we become empowered to stay in control of our lives. Keeping our personal power and being in control of our lives is paramount to reaching total wellness and inner peace.

By engaging in deep reflection, Step 3 also helps us gain insight into how we developed our defense mechanism. This knowledge offers us an opportunity to grow, differentiate ourselves from our parents, and learn better ways to deal with challenging situations and resolve our feelings of annoyance.

The following outlines how we can achieve the stated objectives through the process of self-inquiry:

◊ In general, how do I deal with my feelings of annoyance when people, such as my co-workers, make mistakes? How do I regain my sense of control and inner normalcy when such deep-seated emotions of anger, shame, fear, and anxiety are evoked in me?

◊ Do I treat them as my equal (an imperfect human being) and enlighten them? Or, do I automatically become judgmental and self-righteous (learned behaviors) and treat them as my subordinate in such ways as these:

- » Avoid, snub, or exclude them?
- » Become sarcastic, tease, or ridicule them?
- » Show disdain and contempt (e.g., shake my head, rake my fingers through my hair, give an overpowering stare, or sigh heavily)?
- » Discredit, denigrate, or badmouth them behind their back?
- » Become impatient and snap at them?
- » Raise my voice, speak in an angrily manner, or make rude, hurtful, and belittling remarks?
- » Criticize, reprimand, and demand that they change?
- » Take on the parental responsibilities and over-function (e.g., fix them and tell them what they *should* or *shouldn't* do in an *unsolicited* and condescending manner)?

◊ If yes to any of the above, then how would my behaviors make people like Person B feel? How would I expect them to deal with their own negative emotional experience and respond to me?

◊ If they become defensive and respond negatively to my reactions, then would I *also* take things personally and perceive their hurtful behavior as a judgment, punishment, or rejection of me as a person?

◊ Or, would I see their reaction as their defense mechanism and a rejection of my hurtful behavior?

◊ If I also take things personally and feel victimized, then how do I deal with my painful emotions? Do I use such a defense mechanism as avoidance (e.g., binge eating or drinking) or resistance (e.g., denying, rationalizing, or blaming) to gain a sense of inner normalcy? If yes, then do I see my part in my own emotional suffering?

◊ How did I learn my conditioned defense mechanism?

As mentioned earlier, experts hypothesize that we learn our behaviors and coping strategies during the early years of our childhood as we interact with our immediate environment. This understanding offers us an opportunity to transform and become the person we were born to be. (Refer to *Building a Strong Sense of Self: Embarking on the Journey of Change* for more information on this subject.)

Working through the past three steps of the process of genuine accountability has enabled us to gain insight into our feelings and patterns of inner thoughts and behaviors. Now, we may have a better understanding as to why we become annoyed and how the character flaws that we learned during the early years of our childhood creates emotional suffering. The outline below summarizes these findings:

1. In general, we may feel annoyed when someone's way of thinking, feeling, or behaving triggers memories of aversive events from the past and makes us experience fear and anxiety.

   For example, in the case study that we are exploring in this chapter, we feel annoyed because our co-worker's mistake:

   » *Deviates from our standards of perfection or flawlessness*— This deviation generates anxiety (i.e., *fears of imperfection and others' judgment, rejection, and abandonment*) when we grow up learning that our value or worth, as a person, is based on such factors as the level of our competence or accomplishments; or,

» *Deviates from our social norms*—This deviation generates anxiety (i.e., *fear of other people's judgment, rejection, and abandonment*) when we grow up learning to define our value, as a person, based on how the people in our environment think of us; or,

» *Disrupts our daily routine (or rituals)*—This deviation generates anxiety (i.e., *fear of loss of control*) when we grow up needing a sense of certainty, familiarity, or predictability to feel safe and gain inner normalcy.

Table 10 offers a brief exploration of some other situations in which we feel annoyed by people's character traits (i.e., their ways of thinking, feeling, and behaving).

2. Our negative emotions and feelings that are generated by our distorted realities trigger a series of conditioned and automatic responses (i.e., a set of behaviors that we learned in the early years of our childhood to help us deal with our unpleasant emotions). For example, we may guilt or shame others in order to control their ways of thinking, feeling, or behaving. In essence, then, we unconsciously or consciously try to change others' character traits in order to gain a sense of inner normalcy.

3. These maladaptive coping behaviors result in negative outcomes (i.e., people will avoid us) and emotional suffering (i.e., depression and anxiety).

Table 10

- » When we *need* people to see that we are worthy, we may easily become self-conscious and feel annoyed when others think, feel, or behave in a certain way. In such situations, we become annoyed because we are redirecting our own feelings of anxiety that are generated by our deep-seated *fears of other people's disapproval, rejection, and abandonment.*

- » When we *need* others to see that we are important, we may easily become frustrated and feel annoyed when people's way of thinking, feeling, or behaving doesn't meet our expectations or wishes. In such situations, we become annoyed because we are redirecting our own feelings of anxiety that are generated by our deep-seated *fears of being judged as insignificant and rejected and abandoned.*

- » When we follow a set of binary-based rules (i.e., have a black-and-white or right-and-wrong thinking pattern), we may easily become angry and feel annoyed when people's way of thinking, feeling, or behaving deviates from our rigid standards. In such situations, we become annoyed because we are redirecting our own feelings of anxiety that are generated by our deep-seated *fears of punishment or future mishap.*

- » When we cannot relate to other people's experiences, we may easily become irritated and feel annoyed when others' ways of thinking, feeling, or behaving deviate from our realm of understanding. In such situations, we become annoyed because we are redirecting our own feelings of anxiety that are generated by our deep-seated *fears of the unknown and lack of control.*

- » When we are not emotionally resilient, we may easily become overwhelmed and feel resentful and annoyed when others think, feel, or behave in a certain way—For example, when they speak directly and straightforwardly of a harsh truth that is difficult for us to hear (Figure 1). In such a situation as this, we become annoyed because we are redirecting our own feelings of anxiety that are generated by our deep-seated fears (such as our *fears of powerlessness, breakdown, loss of control, or inadequacy*).

Figure 1

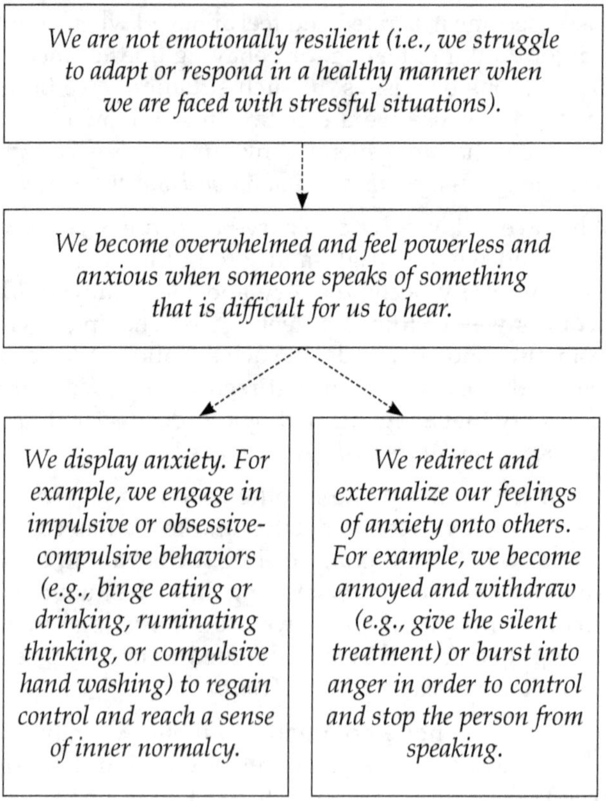

We are not emotionally resilient (i.e., we struggle to adapt or respond in a healthy manner when we are faced with stressful situations).

We become overwhelmed and feel powerless and anxious when someone speaks of something that is difficult for us to hear.

We display anxiety. For example, we engage in impulsive or obsessive-compulsive behaviors (e.g., binge eating or drinking, ruminating thinking, or compulsive hand washing) to regain control and reach a sense of inner normalcy.

We redirect and externalize our feelings of anxiety onto others. For example, we become annoyed and withdraw (e.g., give the silent treatment) or burst into anger in order to control and stop the person from speaking.

The following questions will take us to the fourth step of the process of genuine accountability:

◊ Now that I have discovered the root cause of my negative feelings and emotional suffering then what are my choices?

◊ How can I regain my control and sense of inner normalcy without jeopardizing my relationships or compromising my inner peace?

Step 4

Working through this final step of the genuine accountability process empowers us to deal with our feelings of anxiety and resentment and reach a state of equanimity through making constructive changes: We turn our negative ways of thinking and automatic ways of behaving into constructive self-talks and well-thought-out coping strategies.

Through continue exploring the case study, *I feel annoyed when my co-worker (Person B) makes a mistake*, the following internal contemplations demonstrates how we can achieve this goal:

◊ Seeing my part in my emotional suffering empowers me to regain my personal power. This sense of inner control helps me stay calm and non-reactive and consider such options as:

   A. *Avoid* the source of stress: Distance myself or cut off from Person B whose way of thinking, feeling, and behaving annoys me;

   B. *Accept*: Acknowledge Person B's uniqueness and human-ness, see their *Total Self* (their *weaknesses, limitations, and strengths*), and let them be who they are; and/or,

C. *Change* my character flaws (i.e., *my weaknesses*): Cultivate a set of sound principles that generate constructive and healthy ways of thinking, feeling, and behaving (coping).

◊ After thinking things through and considering the possible outcomes and consequences associated with each of the options, I will arrive at the following conclusions:

» While avoidance may offer emotional relief in the short term, it may not be the best choice in the long run since it will not resolve my issue—I will most likely continue to face similar experiences.

» Furthermore, when it is unwarranted, by cutting off or distancing myself from Person B, I may deprive myself of rewarding experiences and opportunities.

» Therefore, I will choose the combination of the options B and C. Thus, I will:
- Accept Person B's humanness (i.e., their imperfections);
- Better myself by adopting sound values, standards, and virtues that generate positive attitudes and drive healthy coping strategies for dealing with fear and anxiety; and,
- Revisit the past and find inner peace.

◊ When I acknowledge and accept Person B's humanness, then I will not expect them to be perfect. This realistic outlook will help me stay understanding, calm, and non-reactive.

◊ When I cultivate a mindset that is founded on such sound principles as separateness (*we are unique and separate*), empathy, equality, and tolerance, then I will change the way I think and perceive reality.

◊ A pragmatic outlook will help me realize that Person B has a right to their own ways of feeling, thinking, and behaving. Such a constructive state of mind will empower me to stay separate and maintain healthier personal boundaries with Person B (and others). See Appendix 2: *Personal Boundary*.

◊ Adopting an empathetic mindset will empower me to better understand and relate to Person B's experiences and harbor healthier attitudes towards them (and other people who make mistakes).

◊ A positive outlook will drive healthy behaviors and coping strategies and help me experience a more rewarding relationship with Person B (and my other co-workers).

◊ As I gain more awareness and become more mindful, I will be empowered to regulate my emotions and control my impulses.

◊ When I build emotional resilience and learn healthier and more effective ways to deal with my deep-seated fears and anxiety, I will become empowered to revisit the past, gain emotional healing, build a healthy sense of my identity, and harbor healthier attitudes towards myself (refer to *The Inner Control is the True Control Workbook, Second Edition,* for reaching emotional healing).

In summary, when we accept others' humanness, acknowledge their uniqueness, and change the way we think and perceive reality, then we will be empowered to stay separate, tolerant, and non-judgmental in our relationships, be in control of our lives, and experience a state of equanimity and inner harmony. This state of being will lead to rewarding outcomes and a sense of total wellness.

True acceptance is not passive; it is proactive.

*When we acknowledge and accept people's
"humanness and uniqueness"
we become empowered to see their "Total Self"
(i.e., their weaknesses, limitations, and strengths).*

*Such a genuine acceptance that
empowers us to be and let others be
frees us to work on our own weaknesses,
better ourselves, and gain a true sense of inner peace.*

Mindfulness Scripts

> *Please pause a moment, take a few slow and deep breaths, and then read this script aloud.*

During the early years of my life, I looked at my parents and saw my image through their eyes: I saw someone who was special, important, superior and more capable than others (i.e., my siblings).

I received praise and was given a lot of attention for my accomplishments or for solving problems, helping, and taking care of others (i.e., my siblings and parents).

Naturally, I grew up needing to maintain my status (my false sense of identity) in order to gain a sense of inner normalcy (*I am good enough*).

As a result, I adopted a rigid and perfectionistic mindset (an all-or-none attitude): I expected from myself to reach perfection in everything that I did.

In other words, I needed to be always right, be all knowing, win, lead and dominate others to feel that I was worthy and adequate.

As I imposed my perfectionism onto others, I expected people to be perfect.

When others deviated from my standards, I became anxious and felt irritated and annoyed.

Being on autopilot, I disciplined and controlled people so that they met my high standards (i.e., I criticized, fixed, punished, and demanded that they think, feel, or behave in a certain way to meet my unrealistic expectations).

Now that I have built a healthy sense of my self-identity, I understand that I don't have to be perfect, receive praise, be right, be all knowing, fix people, or take care of others in order to be adequate—because, I *am* good enough.

This insight into myself liberates me.
Now, I accept my humanness.

Facing and accepting my human imperfections empowers me to forgive myself for not knowing any better when I mindlessly crossed other people's boundaries to control, fix, or change them. I realize that these automatic behaviors, which I learned in the early years of my life, may have made them feel inadequate.

As I extend my awareness and understanding mindset towards other people, I acknowledge that no one is perfect.

This insight into others liberates me.
Now, I accept other people's humanness.

> *Please stay in the present moment!*

Part III - Chapter Five

> *Our imperfections and mistakes don't define us or devalue us, as a person.*

> *Establishing a set of logical and reasonable expectations for ourselves that are based on excellence and not perfection will liberate us and set us free.*

> "What is stress?
> It's the gap between our expectations and reality.
> More the gap, the more the stress.
> So expect nothing and accept everything."
> —Anonymous

> "In order to change the nature of things, either within yourself or in others, one should change, not the events, but those thoughts which created those events."
> —Leo Tolstoy

> *Please pause a moment, take a few slow and deep breaths, and then read this script aloud.*

During the early years of my childhood, I looked up to my parents and learned about their opinions, beliefs, and values.

Believing that these ways of thinking were the absolute norm, I adopted them as my own.

Since I remained unaware, I grew up learning to evaluate people and appraise their character traits (their ways of thinking, feeling, and behaving) based on these standards that were projected onto me.

When I couldn't understand or relate to others, whose thoughts, feelings, or actions didn't reflect *the Norm*, I became anxious and felt frustrated and annoyed.

Being on autopilot, I became intolerant: I judged them (i.e., labeled them as inferior or inadequate) and punished them (i.e., rejected and abandoned them) to gain a sense of inner normalcy.

This self-discovery humbles me.

Facing and accepting my humanness empowers me to forgive myself for not knowing any better when I mindlessly crossed people's boundaries to fix, change, or control them. I realize that these automatic behaviors, which I learned in the early years of my life, may have made them feel anxious, controlled, and inadequate.

I now understand that, as a mature adult, I can *unlearn*

what I learned: I *can* choose to change my ways of thinking by adopting a new set of principles and standards.

Thus, I no longer need to control people to gain a sense of inner normalcy. Now, I control my inner thoughts and dialogues, instead.

> *Please stay in the present moment!*

Tolerance doesn't mean appeasing others;
Nor does it mean stopping ourselves from
expressing our views or asserting our rights.

Tolerance is about letting go of our feelings of
annoyance so that we could contain the
urge to fix or control other people.

Source: *A Tool for Letting Go of Resentment and Anger: Short. Straightforward. Transformative*.

Would I be more tolerant and accepting of other people (given that they wouldn't violate my personal rights) if I get to know them?

> *Let us define our 'Self' by a set of constructive and sound standards and values that fit our 'True Self.'*
>
> *Let us not allow other people's standards or values to define, control, or limit us.*
>
> Source: <u>A Tool for Letting Go of Resentment and Anger</u>: <u>Short. Straightforward. Transformative</u>.

Part III - Chapter Five

> *Please pause a moment, take a few slow and deep breaths, and then read this script aloud.*

During the early years of my childhood, I not only needed shelter, food, and water, but also needed to be loved unconditionally and to live in a safe and stable environment.

Naturally, as a helpless being, I looked to my caregivers (i.e., parents or parent figures) for those basic human needs.

However, my caregivers weren't able to provide me with adequate warmth, stability, or physical/emotional protection as they had limited *internal* resources.

Unequipped with a more sophisticated coping strategy to deal with my feelings of anxiety, I used my instinctive defense mechanism or adopted the coping behaviors that were role-modeled for me by my caregivers to gain a sense of inner normalcy.

For instance, I learned that playing in a secret place helped me gain a sense of control and safety; or, I discovered that by maintaining structure or order in my environment (i.e., my play) I could escape the present reality that I couldn't control or predict.

As I transitioned into adulthood and remained unaware, I continued to automatically and mindlessly control my environment (i.e., other people's ways of thinking, feeling, or behaving) to reach a sense of inner security and normalcy.

When I was unable to control my environment (i.e., when people deviated from perfection, order, or precision), I became anxious and felt irritated and annoyed.

Being on autopilot, I over-functioned to fix, change, and control things (i.e., I judged, criticized, and demanded that others think, feel, or behave in a way that was strictly consistent with the rules, principles, and code of ethics and conduct).

Acknowledging and accepting my humanness empowers me to forgive myself for not knowing any better when I mindlessly crossed others' personal boundaries to control them. I now understand that these automatic behaviors that I learned in the early years of my life may have made others feel anxious, stressed, and inadequate.

Facing my humanness, taking responsibility for my wrongdoings, and forgiving myself for not knowing any better empower me to relate to other people's humanness and remember that, in the real world, no one is perfect. This knowledge enables me to forgive my caregivers for their wrongdoings or shortcomings during the years that they were raising me.

Holding myself accountable for my own part in my emotional suffering liberates and empowers me to see choices.

As I release my feelings of resentment and take responsibility for my ways of thinking, feeling, and behaving, I gain control over my life.

> *Please stay in the present moment!*

PART III - CHAPTER FIVE

> *To adjust to changes in your environment,*
> *connect with your heart, not your mind.*
> *The compassion in your heart brings you inner peace,*
> *while the thoughts in your mind evoke fear of*
> *the unknown and generate feelings of anxiety*
> *and resentment (i.e., annoyance).*

*The inner control is the true control:
Gaining control over our thoughts and self-talks will empower us to see choices (e.g., set and maintain healthy personal boundaries) and gain control over our lives.*

Source: <u>A Tool for Letting Go of Resentment and Anger: Short. Straightforward. Transformative</u>.

> *Please pause a moment, take a few slow and deep breaths, and then read this script aloud.*

In sum,

My self-discoveries empower me to understand how my own flawed ways of thinking, feeling, and behaving, which I learned during the early years of my childhood, have contributed to my negative emotional experiences.

Now, I realize that I feel annoyed when people think, feel, or behave in a way that evokes memories of aversive events from the past and makes me experience fear and anxiety.

Being on autopilot, I become reactive in such situations: I mindlessly act upon my feelings in a maladaptive manner.

In other words, I *unconsciously* allow the *subconscious emotions of fear and anxiety* to drive a series of conditioned and automatic responses that I learned in the early years of my childhood to help me deal with stressful or unpleasant circumstances.

Naturally, people, in particular, those who have remained unaware, take my behaviors personally and judge, reject, and abandon me.

The truth liberates me:
Now, I see choices.

> *Please stay in the present moment!*

During the early years of our childhood, we naturally experience fear and automatically exhibit anxiety when we are faced with stressful or undesirable situations.

When our immediate environment (i.e., parent or parent figure) over-functions for us (i.e., overprotective parenting), then we don't learn to deal with our unpleasant emotions (i.e., anxiety) in those challenging times.

In such a case as this, we learn to continue to express our feelings of anxiety outwardly in order to stop and control the stressors that trigger our inner unrest. That is to say, we learn to display signs of anxiety (i.e., become annoyed) as a way to control our environment—events that we find overwhelming or unpleasant).

In essence, by exhibiting anxiety, we are saying, "I feel helpless."

When such a dynamic pattern remains unchecked, our defensive behaviors become conditioned in us as we transition into adulthood.

As adults, when the associative part of our brain is triggered by a stressor (i.e., an event that we find overwhelming or undesirable), our emotional brain generates the same emotional response as when we were a child: The stimulus (i.e., the event) evokes the emotion of fear, generates feelings of anxiety, and drives anxious behaviors.

In other words, when we remain unaware, we may not even realize that the Child in us exhibits anxiety during times of stress in order to control the environment and gain a sense of inner normalcy.

6

I Feel Jealous

This chapter explores a hypothetical case study in which we are experiencing resentment towards someone because we are feeling jealous. Some examples of such a situation would be when we are bitter and resentful because we view others as being more successful, accomplished, intelligent, attractive, or popular than us.

The remainder of this chapter demonstrates how working through the four steps of the process of genuine accountability empowers us to deal with our feelings of jealousy without compromising our relationships or inner peace. In order to better understand the process, we focus on a scenario in which we are jealous because someone, such as our friend, is thinner or more physically fit than us: *I feel jealous because my friend is more physically fit than me.*

I Feel Jealous Because My Friend (Referred to as 'Person C') Is More Physically Fit Than Me

Step 1

As the first step in the process of genuine accountability, we acknowledge all of our negative feelings towards Person C (e.g., envy, bitterness, anger, disgust, and/or hatred).

It is important to keep in mind that *all* of the emotions that one can feel is a natural part of the human experience. Therefore, our feelings of jealousy are all real, valid, and acceptable.

Our negative emotions only become dysfunctional when we act upon them (a reactionary response), rather than resolving them.

This non-judgmental acknowledgment of our feelings directs our attention to the root cause of our emotional experience: our mindset. Thus, we refocus and become aware of our internal thoughts and dialogues that generate our feelings of jealousy without being self-deprecating or self-critical.

Step 2

When we realize that we are bitter and resentful because we are jealous of Person C's physical appearance, we ask ourselves the following thought-provoking questions in order to gain insight into our inner thoughts, self-talks, and deep-seated emotions that generate our feelings of jealousy. The knowledge that we gain through this self-inquiry process enables us to discover the truth—the root cause of our negative emotional experience.

◊ Why am I jealous of Person C's physical appearance? What are my internal thoughts?

◊ Do I think that Person C is better, superior, or more special than me since they are more fit? In other words, do I think that I'm inferior or that I'm not good enough because I'm not fit (or that I'm not as fit as Person C is)?

◊ If yes, then is it possible that, at the subconscious level, such a distorted reality (*"I'm not good enough ... I'm inferior"*) triggers a perception of threat to my sense of identity, as a person (*"I am better than others ... I am more special than others"*)?

◊ If so, then could my false perception evoke the deep-seated emotion of shame and generate feelings of anxiety (fearing others' judgment, rejection, or abandonment)?

◊ In other words, do I experience feelings of jealousy and resentment because, subconsciously, I am projecting my own feelings of disappointment, shame, and anxiety (*"I'm not better ... Others like Person C more ... I'm inadequate"*) onto Person C?

◊ If yes, then why? Why do I need to be physically fit to think that I'm good enough? Why do I need to be superior or better than others to feel good about myself? Why do I need other people's affirmation to think that I'm adequate?

◊ Could it be because I define my value, as a person, based on external factors, such as my physical appearance, popularity, and what other people think of me?

◊ If yes, then do I find myself constantly comparing myself to others? Do I become competitive in most areas of my life, such as in my relationships or career?

◊ If yes, then do I frequently experience feelings of jealousy and resentment towards people whom I perceive as being better than me?

◊ If so, then do I regularly suffer from mood swings? If yes, then could this be because my sense of self-identity or self-value changes from moment to moment (i.e., I become overly excited and self-congratulatory when I receive attention or praise from others at work; the next day, I experience self-doubt and depressed moods when one of my coworkers gets more attention than I do)?

◊ If yes, then how did I learn to define or evaluate my self-value in such a way? I know that I was not born with my ways of thinking, so how did I learn them?

◊ As a child, did I receive preferential treatment from one or both of my parents or parent figures? If yes, then did I grow up considering myself as being more special than others (i.e., my siblings)? In other words, did I grow up needing to be superior or better than others in order to gain a sense of inner normalcy?

◊ Moreover, did I receive preferential treatment as a child but lost it to someone else later on (i.e., at the arrival of a younger sibling or a step-parent)?

◊ Was I raised in a household where people (e.g., my parents) constantly compared themselves with others? If yes, then did they constantly worry about how others viewed them? If yes, then did they see me as their extension—a reflection on them—and worried about how people in their social circle would view me? Was I compared with other children? In other words, as a child, did I learn to build my personal identity based on such external factors as what others thought of me?

◊ During the early years of my childhood, did I receive a lot of praise for my physical attributes? Did I learn to think that I had to be special (i.e., good looking and fit) to think that I was adequate? In other words, as a child, did I learn to build my personal identity based on such external factors as my appearance?

Having gained insight into our mindset, we may now understand how the principles, values, and standards that we acquired during the early years of our childhood play a key role in our negative emotional experiences.

Step 3

In this step of the process of genuine accountability, we focus on our automatic behaviors (our conditioned defense mechanisms): We observe ourselves in a non-judgmental and calm manner and become aware of our patterns of behavioral response that are driven by our feelings of jealousy and negative inner thoughts and self-talks.

Moreover, we observe others (i.e., Person C) in a non-judgmental manner and understand how our automatic behaviors make them feel and respond to us.

The knowledge that we gain through these observations allows us to discover our part in our emotional suffering.

Holding ourselves accountable for our own part in our unhappiness empowers us to keep our personal power and be in control of our own lives—which is paramount to reaching total wellness and inner peace.

Lastly, we discover how we developed our conditioned defense mechanisms as we engage in deep reflection in this step of the process of genuine accountability. This insight offers us the opportunity to grow, transform, and learn better ways to deal with our feelings of jealousy.

The following demonstrates how we reach our objectives through the process of self-inquiry:

- How do I generally deal with my negative inner thoughts and feelings when I become jealous of others? Do I automatically:
  - Become competitive?
  - Become possessive?
  - Externalize my deep-seated emotion of shame and feelings of jealousy? For example, would I snub the people that I'm jealous of? Would I show contempt? Would I ridicule them? Would I tease them? Would I become sarcastic? Would I find faults with them? Would I belittle or denigrate them? Would I sabotage them?
- If yes, then how do I expect those people (i.e., Person C) to deal with their feelings of hurt, anger, and resentment?
- If they have remained unaware and respond to my hurtful behaviors in an automatic and reactive manner, then how do I deal with my hurtful feelings?
- Do I see their reactions as *their* defense mechanism and a rejection of *my behavior*? Do I hold myself accountable for my own part and resolve the issue appropriately and effectively?
- Or, do I take things personally and perceive their reactive behaviors towards me as a rejection of *Me*—as a person?
- If so, then do I feel victimized?
- If yes, then how do I cope with my inner turmoil? For instance, do I engage in self-pity and seek comfort in alcohol, food, or other substances?
- If yes, then how did I learn such coping behaviors?

As mentioned earlier, experts hypothesize that we learn our behaviors and defense mechanisms during the early years of our childhood as we interact with our immediate environment. (For more information on this subject, refer to *Building a Strong Sense of Self: Embarking on the Journey of Change*.)

Working through the past three steps of the genuine accountability process has enabled us to discover our truth: the faulty patterns of our thoughts and behaviors that we learned in the early years of our childhood (i.e., to protect us against emotional pain) have led to negative emotional experiences and suffering (Table 11).

Table 11

I Feel Jealous

In the early years of my childhood, I received preferential treatment, were overly attended to, or received a lot of praise;
↓
Therefore, I grew up perceiving myself as being superior, more important, or more special than other people;
↓
Having remained unaware, I constantly needed to be better than others in order to gain a sense of inner normalcy—a reaffirmation of the sense of my value as a person;
↓
Thus, I constantly compared myself with other people;
↓
I felt inadequate and inferior when I perceived someone else (e.g., a friend or coworker) as being better than me: *"I'm not good enough;"*
↓
At the subconscious level, my distorted reality evoked the deep-seated emotions of shame and anxiety (i.e., fears of others' judgment) and triggered a perception of threat to my false sense of identity: *"I am not superior, special, or more important;"*
↓

> **Table 11**
>
> ### I Feel Jealous (Cont'd)
>
> I developed feelings of jealousy, resentment, and animosity towards the person;
>
> ↓
>
> Unable to deal with my inner turmoil (a lack of resilience), I externalized my unbearable feelings (e.g., I became passive-aggressive and denigrated or badmouthed the person);
>
> ↓
>
> The individual took things personally, felt victimized, and responded in reactive manner (e.g., they became passive-aggressive and avoided me);
>
> ↓
>
> I felt rejected: "*I am not good enough.*"

Our self-discovery is liberating and empowering since it helps us to see that we are not stuck: we *can* have different emotional experiences when we choose to commit ourselves to *unlearning* what we have learned.

The following question takes us to the fourth and final step of the genuine accountability process—the path towards positive life experiences:

◊ How can I take control, transform, and reach inner peace?

Step 4

The internal contemplations that are outlined below will demonstrate how we overcome our feelings of jealousy, make constructive changes, and reach equanimity in this final step of the genuine accountability process.

We achieve these objectives as we continue to explore the hypothetical case study, *"I feel jealous because my friend (Person C) is more physically fit than me."*

◊ Having discovered my part in my emotional suffering, I now see that I *can* have a different emotional experience in my relationship with Person C.

◊ This sense of personal power and control empowers me to consider such options as the following:

   A. *Avoid* the source of stress: Cut off or distance myself from Person C, whom I see as better or more special than me;

   B. *Accept:* Acknowledge my humanness and affirm my *Total Self* (*my strengths, weaknesses, and limitations*)—Cherish my *strengths* with gratitude, accept my *limitations* with equanimity and serenity, and improve my *weaknesses* (i.e., my present level of physical fitness) with firm commitment and resilience; and/or,

   C. *Change* my character flaws (i.e., *my weaknesses*): Cultivate a set of sound principles that generate constructive and healthy ways of thinking, feeling, and behaving.

◊ After considering all of the possible consequences and outcomes that are associated with each of the above options, I will arrive at the following decision: While avoidance offers emotional relief in the short term, it will neither resolve my issue nor will it generate a sense of inner peace in the long term. Additionally, by avoiding Person C, I may deprive myself of rewarding experiences.

◊ Thus, I will choose the combination of the options B and C:

- » I will affirm myself: "*I am neither inferior nor superior to Person C . . . I am good enough . . . I'm inherently worthy.*"

- » I will stop evaluating myself based on external factors, such as my physical attributes or what others think of me, which evoke negative emotions and generate self-deprecating internal thoughts and maladaptive coping behaviors.

- » Instead, I will develop and cultivate well-thought-out principles that are based on wisdom, logical reasoning, and virtues (e.g., compassion and empathy).

- » I will allow these principles (internal factors) to serve as a foundation on which I build and define my sense of self-identity and evaluate my self-value.

- » Accordingly, I will work on my weaknesses by setting goals that are based on such sound principles (i.e., I will work on becoming physically fit because I would like to *improve my health*).

- » I will make concrete plans and commit to them to meet my goals.

◊ When I accept my humanness and adopt a constructive mindset that fosters positive attitudes towards myself, then I will harbor such self-talks as these: "*My body weight or the level of my physical fitness does not define me. I don't have to be better, thinner, or more physically fit than Person C to be adequate. I am good enough.*"

◊ Such nurturing internal thoughts and dialogues will generate positive feelings and healthy behaviors (i.e., responsible self-care).

◊ As I maintain a healthy lifestyle and achieve my goals, I will become happier and more self-confident. When I am happy, I will be able to have rewarding experiences with Person C and enjoy better emotional and physical health.

In summary, when we change our faulty ways of thinking by adopting sound principles, then we will evaluate our *'Self'* based on constructive standards. This positive state of mind will empower us to be self-confident, feel secure in our relationships, and experience a sense of inner harmony and total wellness.

> *While I cherish my strengths and take pride in my accomplishments, I realize that my advantages, greatness, gifts, talents, or skills do not define me or make me superior.*
>
> *While I support myself in turning my weaknesses into my strengths, I realize that my imperfections, flaws, or limitations do not define me or make me inferior.*
>
> Source: <u>Building a Strong Sense of Self: Embarking on the Journey of Change</u>

A Mindfulness Script

> Please pause a moment, take a few slow and
> deep breaths, and then read this script aloud.

During the early years of my childhood, I looked at my parent and saw myself in her eyes as being *the favorite child*.

Naturally, I grew up needing to keep this status in the eyes of others and be *everyone's favorite* in order to find inner normalcy—think that I was good enough.

When I found myself being replaced by other people (i.e., a younger sibling, another coworker, or a step-parent), I developed feelings of jealousy and inadequacy.

In such situations, my distorted reality (i.e., *I am being robbed of my rights*) led me to think that I was being victimized. So, I became angry and resentful.

Being on autopilot, I expressed my animosity and hostility towards those people in an aggressive or passive-aggressive manner.

Now that I have gained insight into myself, I can easily see that there is no path to total wellness when I measure my value, as a person, based on what other people think of me (i.e., my popularity level):

> *Do they like me?*
> *Am I their favorite?*

Now, I have learned to evaluate myself based on internal factors (e.g., honesty, compassion, and empathy).

Now, I allow such sound standards to govern my inner thoughts, feelings, and behaviors.

This constructive mindset generates nurturing and responsible self-talks. As a result, I no longer swing from:

> A state of mind in which I perceive myself as
> being inadequate and helpless
> (i.e., when I'm not liked or favored over others),
> To
> A state of mind in which I perceive myself as
> being superior and entitled
> (i.e., when I'm admired or favored over others).

Now, I know that we are all equal. Thus, I no longer put myself, or anyone else, on the pedestal.

The realization that we are equal and therefore we are all equally imperfect helps me to see that:

> We all have our own sets of strengths,
> weaknesses, and limitations.

This insight stops me from comparing myself.

Now, I don't need to be the favorite or be liked by everyone to think that I am adequate:

> *Now, I know that I-am-adequate.*

Now that I assume an equal posturing in my interactions with other people, I am empowered to connect with them on a deeper level and enjoy *positive emotional experiences*.

> Please stay in the present moment!

PART III - CHAPTER SIX

What consumes your mind controls your life.
—Anonymous

> *Do we end up punishing ourselves when we redirect our own feelings of jealousy onto others?*

> *How do we deal with the natural human emotion of jealousy?*
>
> *Do we allow our feelings of envy or jealousy to control our lives?*
>
> *Or, do we retake our control and choose to be inspired by people whom we feel envious of?*
>
> *We always have a choice.*
>
> Source: <u>A Tool for Letting Go of Resentment and Anger: Short. Straightforward. Transformative</u>.

Part III - Chapter Six

> *When we define our self-image based on the concept of exceptionalism—we need to be better, superior, or more special than others to be good enough—then we have to constantly compare ourselves with other people to make sure that we 'are' better, superior, or more special than them.*
>
> Source: <u>A Tool for Letting Go of Resentment and Anger: Short. Straightforward. Transformative.</u>

> Would we be less resentful of others if we loved ourselves more?
>
> Would we love ourselves more if we experience more rewarding relationships?

> To discover your 'true Self' and love yourself unconditionally, make peace with your past.

7
I Feel That I Have Been Wronged

> ### A Word of Caution!
>
> *Please be informed that this chapter is not designed for the victims of rape or sexual assault or for those individuals who were physically or sexually abused as children.*
>
> *While working through this chapter may help, seeking professional support and guidance is strongly recommended for reaching a true state of emotional healing in such cases.*

This chapter explores a hypothetical case study in which we experience intense resentment because we were wronged by someone and therefore, we feel hurt, attacked, or violated.

By working through the four steps of the process of genuine accountability, this section demonstrates how, in such a situation as this, we can overcome our feelings of resentment, resolve issues, and move onward and upward.

Step 1

As the first step in the process of genuine accountability, we identify, acknowledge and validate our painful feelings (e.g., violated, victimized, demeaned, rejected, humiliated, unloved, numb, helpless, stuck, sad, anger, rage, and/or hatred) without being judgmental, blaming, or critical towards ourselves.

Realizing that we have no control over other people's ways of thinking, feeling, or behaving, we focus on ourselves and explore our choices to find emotional relief and to ensure that we wouldn't be victimized again. Identifying and owning our feelings is the key to keeping our personal power, seeing options, and maintaining control over our lives.

Step 2

As we connect with our inner selves and go through the process of introspection, we gain insight into our deep-seated emotions, inner thoughts, and self-talks that are triggered by others' abusive behaviors. This knowledge enables us to understand what happened so that we could make better decisions.

We start this step by asking ourselves: *"What makes me feel that I was violated?"* In other words: *"How was I wronged?"* The following outlines the thought-provoking questions that we ask of ourselves in order to discover the truth:

◊ How was I wronged? I realize that I, like others, deserve to be treated with dignity (i.e., with respect, equality, equity, and fairness). Was any of my basic human rights (mindlessly or intentionally) violated by the individual?

» Were my *physical rights* violated?
For example, was my body, physical space, physical privacy, or personal space (including the food that I eat or the attire or make-up that I wear) violated?

» Were my *verbal rights* (my freedom of speech) violated?
Was I stopped from expressing my thoughts, feelings, opinions, hopes, or desires? For example, was I silenced through such behaviors as domination or intimidation (i.e., screamed at, snapped at, or interrupted) when I shared my realities, feelings, or honest opinions; verbalized my hopes, desires, or needs; or, asked questions?

» Were my *mental or emotional rights* violated?
For example, were my thoughts, realities, or feelings dismissed, neglected, ridiculed, or degraded?
Was I demanded of?
Was I threatened?
Was I controlled or manipulated through humiliation and shaming?
Was I controlled, pressured, or coerced to conformity through guilting?
Was I retaliated against or punished (e.g., badmouthed or given the silent treatment) when I asserted myself?
Was I the victim of smearing or gossiping?
Was I lied to or betrayed?
Was my trust betrayed by broken commitments?
Was I blamed, guilted, shamed, or demeaned for the person's own feelings of anxiety, stress, frustration, jealousy, shame, or guilt? For instance:
- Was I shouted at or snapped at because the person was having a bad day?

- Was I sabotaged (i.e., victimized in a subtle manner) because the person became jealous and resentful of me for receiving more attention?
- Was I treated with hostility because the person felt offended by my feedback or opinion? Was I blamed, shamed, or guilted since they felt inferior or inadequate when I held them accountable for their wrongdoings?
- Was I scorned and treated with contempt, disgust, or disdain because the person felt annoyed when I made a mistake or asked questions?

» Were my *material rights* violated?
For example, were my belongings (e.g., cell phone, computer, or clothes) used or taken away without my permission or full consent?
Were my possessions or physical environment mindlessly or deliberately damaged or vandalized?

» Were my *sexual rights* violated?
For instance, were my rights to make such decisions as how, when, where, and with whom to have sexual activity violated?

» Were my *spiritual rights* violated?
For example, were my religious or spiritual values, beliefs, or practices ridiculed, dismissed, degraded, or silenced?

To better understand the role that the process of genuine accountability plays in reaching emotional healing, we focus on the following hypothetical case study while we continue to work our way through the second step: *"I feel emotionally hurt because my spouse tends to take their stress out on me."*

> *Verbal Rights:*
> *Am I infringing on other people's emotional rights if my speech vilifies, discriminates, divides, or spreads hatred?*

> *When "one's rights" infringe on our "physical, verbal, emotional, spiritual, or sexual rights," then, are they "our rights" or, are they "our demands?"*

> *Emotional Rights:*
> *Is everyone worthy of being treated with respect, dignity, and equality, regardless of such factors as their physical characteristics (e.g., skin tone or color, weight, or height), gender, gender identity, sexual orientation, background, intelligence, level of education, wealth, accomplishment, religious or spiritual beliefs, or ways of thinking or feeling about a situation?*

I Feel Emotionally Hurt Because My Spouse (Referred to as 'Person D') Tends to Take Their Stress Out on Me

Step 2 (Cont'd)

While keeping this scenario in mind, we connect with our inner *Self*. Through asking ourselves thought-provoking questions, we gain insight into our conscious and subconscious thoughts and emotions that are triggered by Person D's behavior. The self-inquiry questions that are outlined below demonstrate how we achieve this objective:

◊ Do I take Person D's behavior personally and think to myself: *"I'm being taken for granted; Person D doesn't treat others the way they treat me . . . Person D doesn't love me . . . I'm not important to them . . . I'm not lovable . . . ?"* In other words, could it be that, at the subconscious level, Person D's behavior triggers a perception of threat to my sense of worth, as a person, and creates such a self-image as: *"I don't matter?"*

◊ If so, then could this distorted perception evoke the deep-seated emotions of *shame, fear,* and *guilt* as it triggers such *internal* thoughts and dialogues as: *"I am not a good spouse . . . I'm not worthy of being loved . . . I fear Person D's retaliatory reactions (i.e., abandonment) . . . I should be more tolerant and understanding in order to be good and worthy?"*

◊ If so, then could these conscious or subconscious inner thoughts generate such feelings as self-doubt, anxiety, inner conflict, resentment, helplessness, and being stuck?

◊ If yes, then why? Why do I take Person D's maladaptive coping mechanism (scapegoating) personally and harbor such self-defeating internal thoughts that generate emotional pain?

- Instead, why don't I consider such situations as these: Perhaps, Person D has difficulty regulating their emotions? Maybe, they have a hard time expressing their true feelings to others because they are not self-confident (i.e., Person D fears other people's judgment, rejection, and abandonment)? Or, perhaps, Person D externalizes and redirects their pent-up negative feelings towards me because they see me as being *safe*? In other words, perhaps, I have enabled Person D to see me as a "safe outlet" for releasing their painful emotions (i.e., stress or frustration)?

- Taking this impersonal perspective allows me to refocus and reflect on issues that I have control over. Therefore, while holding Person D accountable for their wrongdoings towards me, I will ask myself: Why have I taken up the role of the scapegoat in my relationship with Person D? Or, to put it differently, why have I allowed Person D (or others) to see me as a "safe outlet" for releasing their painful emotions?

- Could it be because I don't have a healthy sense of my worth, as a person? If yes, then why?

- Could it be because, during the early years of my childhood, I grew up in a household with limited external resources that were necessary for healthy child care and development?

- Or, is it possible that I suffer from a lack of self-worth because, during the early years of my childhood, I was raised by parents or parent figures who were not "awakened" (See Page 13)? For example, could it be that my parents or parent figures were more focused on pleasing others than minding me because they suffered from a lack of self-esteem and feared others' judgment, rejection, or abandonment? Or, could it be that they had trouble regulating their emotions and impulses (because they lacked internal resources—resilience—to face setbacks or challenging situations) and therefore, they took their stress out on me?

◊ In other words, could it be that in the early years of my childhood, I had such experiences as these:
  » I was neglected (i.e., my physical, emotional, or mental needs were ignored)?
  » My opinions, realities, or feelings were dismissed?
  » I was treated differently or valued less than my siblings?
  » I was blamed for others' own mistakes, failures, stress, or frustration?
  » I was physically disciplined or emotionally punished (i.e., demeaned, shamed, scorned, guilted, or given the cold shoulder, or badmouthed) when I asserted myself?
  » I was not protected or defended by my parent(s) when I was victimized (i.e., when one of my parents or an older sibling took their frustration out on me—verbally, physically, or emotionally)?
  » I received acknowledgment or affirmation (i.e., that I was a good child or that I was worthy of love or attention) when I empathized with the feelings or experiences of others in my family (i.e., my parents or siblings), rather than those of my own? In other words, I learned to become more attentive to the needs of other people, even at a cost to myself, so that I would be acknowledged (i.e., recognized) or affirmed that I was a good child?

◊ If yes, then could it be that, at the subconscious level, Person D's behavior triggers a repressed memory of a traumatic or unpleasant event in my childhood?

◊ If so, then could this recovered memory, subconsciously, create the perception of: *I don't matter*? If yes, then does this perception accurately represent the truth?

◊ Moreover, could this recovered memory of childhood trauma, subconsciously, create a perception of threat to my sense of security (i.e., *I fear Person D's abandonment or angry retaliation . . . I'm helpless*)? If so, then could this be why I experience anxiety and feel powerless and stuck? If yes, then does this perception of threat accurately represent the present reality?

◊ Finally, could such internal thoughts and feelings trigger a set of automatic responses (my defense mechanism) in me? This question takes us to the next step.

Step 3

In the third step of the process of genuine accountability, we focus on our automatic behaviors that are driven by our feelings (Step 1) and internal thoughts and self-talks (Step 2). As we continue to observe and reflect on our *Self* in a non-judgmental manner, we become aware of how our pattern of behavioral responses (our defense mechanism) contributes to our emotional suffering.

This self-discovery empowers us to remain in control and change our emotional experiences through adopting healthier ways of protecting our basic human rights—As discussed earlier, our emotional well-being is paramount to reaching total wellness and inner peace.

Additionally, through engaging in deep reflection, Step 3 may also help us find out how we developed our defense mechanism.

This knowledge offers us an opportunity for personal growth and transformation.

The following self-inquiry questions demonstrate how we can achieve these objectives while we continue to focus on the hypothetical case study: *"I feel emotionally hurt because my spouse (Person D) tends to take their stress out on me."*

◊ I understand that, as a mature and capable adult, I am responsible for protecting myself. So, how do I generally tend to guard my basic human rights? How do I reclaim my individuality and protect my personal boundaries in my relationships? How do I defend myself when others (i.e., Person D) violate my personal boundaries (i.e., take their stress out on me and violate my emotional rights)?

◊ Do I remain secure and strong and share my realities, thoughts, and feelings openly and in a non-reactive and non-provocative manner? Do I set appropriate and clear limits in a healthy way? Do I maintain the limits that I set consistently and effectively? If not, then why not?

◊ Could it be because I'm generally unaware of my own feelings, thoughts, or needs? Could it be because I am not cognizant of my own basic human rights? In other words, do I have difficulty protecting myself because I don't have a clear concept of my own personal boundaries in order to set clear and healthy limits in my interactions with others?

◊ Or, could it be that I am aware of my basic human rights and that I set healthy personal boundaries, but I have difficulty *maintaining* them consistently and effectively? For example, is it possible that in my relationship with Person D, I don't stay strong and enforce the limits that I set because I tend to swing from one *state of being* to another in the following manner (see Figure 2 on Page 132):

» *The state of compliance:*
I become overly compliant and attentive to the needs and feelings of Person D and neglect to check in with those of mine (i.e., *I need to be nice, giving, and selfless in order to be good and worthy of love, attention, or taking care of*);

TO

» *The state of passivity:*
I take things personally when Person D treats me poorly (i.e., takes their stress out on me). I become passive, bottle up my feelings of resentment, and withdraw (i.e., *I'm a victim . . . I'm too weak to stand up for myself . . . Poor Me!*);

TO

» *The state of reactivity:*
After reaching my tolerance threshold, I assert myself, set limits, and express my feelings in a reactive and provocative manner (aggressive communications) or express my hurt feelings indirectly, through subtle acts (passive-aggressive communications);

TO

» *The state of anxiety and inner turmoil:*
Soon after calming down, I experience anticipatory anxiety: I start to worry since I expect and fear that Person D would become defensive (e.g., blame, dismiss my reality, or judge me), reactionary (e.g., become loud and aggressive), or retaliatory (e.g., withdraw love or talk about me behind my back in order to recruit others to take side) (i.e., *Person D will punish me . . . give me the cold shoulder . . . badmouth me . . . others will judge and reject me . . .*);

Figure 2

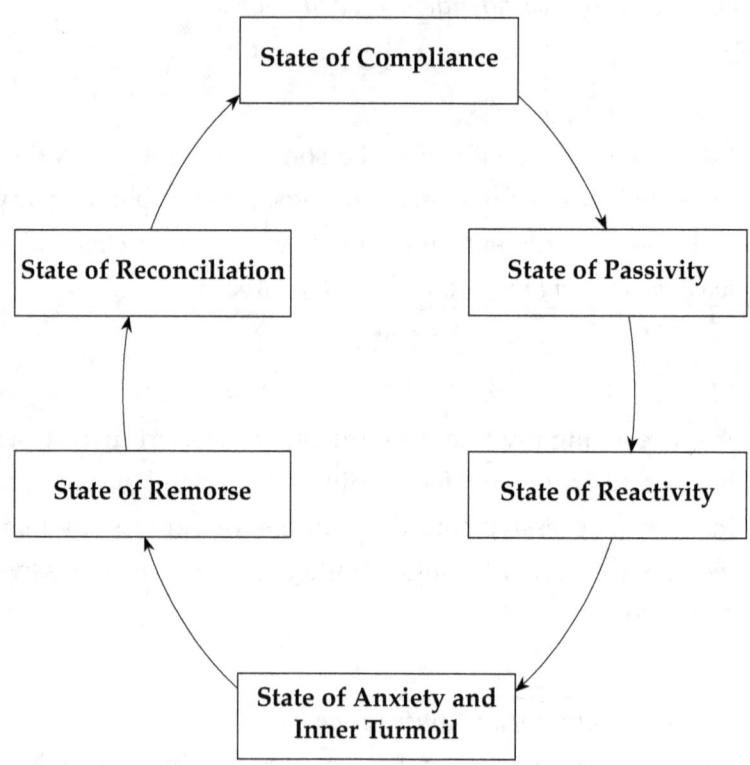

TO

» *The state of remorse:*
I start doubting myself and experiencing the feelings of remorse (shame and guilt). I become self-critical and self-reproachful (i.e., *Maybe, it was all my fault . . . I should have been more understanding . . . I'm not good . . .*);

TO

» *The state of reconciliation:*
I lose my sense of self (loss of individuality) as I over-identify and over-empathize with the experiences and feelings of Person D while neglecting to check in with those of mine. Therefore, without holding Person D accountable for their wrongdoings towards me, I become overly apologetic and conciliatory (i.e., *Person D is going through a rough time and is feeling frustrated . . . Poor them!*);

BACK TO

» *The state of compliance:*
I resume being overly compliant. Consequently, I get stuck in a toxic relationship pattern with Person D (i.e., *I need to get along with Person D in order to be worthy of love*).

◊ If that's the case, then does that mean that I have difficulty maintaining my personal boundaries and protecting myself in my relationships because I tend to be emotionally dependent (i.e., I need other people's approval to gain a sense of self-worth, inner safety, security, and normalcy)?

◊ If yes, then how do I expect to be treated by Person D or others who have remained unawakened (i.e., live on autopilot and are unaware of how their actions violate others' basic human rights) when I set unclear and malleable personal boundaries?

◊ In other words, how do I expect people to respond to me when, in their interactions with me, they experience:

» *A sense of entitlement:*
They see themselves as deserving of special treatment when I become overly compliant and attentive?

» *Confusion and frustration:*
They become frustrated (due to the lack of control) and develop anxiety (due to the deep-seated fears of being rejected and abandoned) when I bottle up my feelings and withdraw?

» *Resentment and anger:*
They feel hurt and victimized when I become responsive and hold them accountable in a reactive manner?

» *Self-pity:*
Seeing themselves as a victim, they develop a *victim mentality*, form grievance stories, and hold grudges against me when I become remorseful and overly apologetic, without holding them accountable for their own wrongdoings?

» *Enabled:*
Being emboldened, they return to their old dysfunctional pattern of behavior (i.e., they mindlessly continue to violate my personal boundaries), while I, instead of setting healthy personal boundaries, return to my own maladaptive way of coping (i.e., I mindlessly continue to take things personally and respond in a passive, aggressive, or passive-aggressive manner)?

◊ To put it differently, how could I expect Person D or others to transform and gain empathy when I enable them? How could I expect them to learn that such behaviors as acting out (i.e., taking their stress out on me) or punishing (i.e., shaming or guilting me into submission) are hurtful and emotionally abusive when I don't hold them accountable in a consistent and appropriate manner?

◊ Moreover, how could I find peace and true happiness if I allow my false sense of identity (low self-worth) and such deep-seated emotions as guilt, shame, fear, or helplessness to take control and stop me from having healthy relationships?

◊ How did I develop my maladaptive patterns of coping with such situations in which my basic human rights are being violated?

◊ Did I learn these self-preservation and defensive behaviors during the early years of my childhood as I interacted with my immediate environment? (For more information on this subject, refer to *Building a Strong Sense of Self: Embarking on the Journey of Change*.)

◊ Are these defense mechanisms being reinforced in me by the type of relationships I have chosen to have? In other words, as an adult, have I repeatedly had relationships in which I have experienced the same dysfunctional relationship dynamics? If yes, then why is that?

◊ Do I now see my own part in my emotional suffering?

※ ※ ※

The following questions will take us to the fourth step of the process of genuine accountability:

◊ Now that I can identify my part in my own emotional suffering then what are my choices?

◊ How can I regain my control, remain non-reactive, stay secure and strong, and set healthy personal boundaries appropriately and effectively in my relationships?

◊ In other words, how can I protect myself, gain a state of equanimity, and enjoy a healthier relationship with Person D?

Step 4

Working through this final step empowers us to: Regain our personal power (*become secure*) by identifying with our own realities and empathizing with our own feelings; reach a state of equanimity (*become non-reactive*) by cultivating an understanding and forgiving mindset; and, take control over our lives (*become strong and proactive*) by making constructive changes (i.e., adopt healthier ways of protecting our basic human rights).

The following internal contemplations demonstrate how we can achieve these objectives as we continue to explore the hypothetical case study, *"I feel emotionally hurt because my spouse (Person D) takes their stress out on me."*

◊ As a mature and capable adult, it is my responsibility to protect and defend myself.

◊ I realize that I cannot control Person D's ways of thinking, feeling, or behaving; therefore, I will focus on those of mine in order to find effective and appropriate ways to stop Person D from mistreating me. This choice offers me a sense of control and empowers me to consider such options as these: I can,

A. *Avoid* the source of stress: Cut off (e.g., divorce) or distance myself from Person D;

B. *Accept:* Let go of my feelings of resentment by accepting our (i.e., Person D's and my own) humanness and *Total Self* (i.e., our strengths, limitations, and weaknesses such as, our faulty patterns of behaviors) with equanimity and empathy; and/or,

C. *Change* my character flaws (i.e., *my weaknesses*): Cultivate a set of sound principles that generate constructive and healthy ways of thinking, feeling, and behaving.

◊ After thinking things through and considering the possible outcomes and consequences associated with each of the options, I will arrive at the following conclusions:

» Cutting off (e.g., divorcing) or distancing myself from Person D will not resolve my issue; unless I transform, I will most likely continue to have similar experiences in my future relationships.

» Moreover, if I take option A without addressing my own issue, I may not be giving my relationship with Person D a fair chance; therefore, I might experience regret in the future.

» Being understanding and accepting of Person D's and my own humanness may help me to let go of my feelings of resentment, but only for a short time: Leading a passive life will not free me from experiencing emotional pain in the long term.

» Furthermore, without learning healthy ways to hold Person D accountable for their wrongdoings towards me, taking option B is not only unhelpful (i.e., it doesn't resolve our issue) but also harmful and unfair to both of us (i.e., it reinforces Person D's maladaptive behaviors and it keeps me from living a dignified life that I'm deserving of).

» Therefore, I will choose the combination of the options B and C at this time: While I accept our humanness with an understanding and forgiving heart, I will commit to fixing my part in our unhealthy relationship dynamic: I will adopt constructive principles that drive healthier patterns of behaviors. If this measure fails to bring about a change in our relationship (i.e., a transformation in Person D), then I will consider the option A and cut off.

◊ When I cultivate a constructive mindset that is founded on sound and constructive principles, then I will have such internal thoughts and dialogues as the following:

Holding myself accountable for my own part in my emotional suffering frees me from seeing myself as a helpless and trapped victim.

Since I no longer wallow in self-pity or engage in obsessive thinking, I become liberated and empowered to refocus: I see Person D's 'Total Self,' upbringing, and past events that have impacted his weaknesses and limitations.

The insight into Person D empowers me to change the way I perceive the present reality: Person D's maladaptive way of dealing with their negative feelings is not about me.

Taking this impersonal view helps me not to take Person D's defense mechanism personally.

It also enables me to see that Person D's behavior is separate from the person they are. This realization empowers me to accept and forgive Person D, but reject their behaviors.

Acceptance and forgiveness bring about a sense of calmness in me.

As I reach a state of equanimity, I gain the ability to access my thinking brain (prefrontal cortex), reflect, and gain a sense of my own self.

Having gained more insight into myself, I now see Me: I matter. I am worthy of love and respect. I believe in myself and my own abilities to protect and defend my basic human rights.

I will not live my life fearing other people's angry or retaliatory responses; nor will I live my life fearing others' judgment, rejection, or abandonment.

I will become secure and trust my own judgment. I will stay strong and become proactive: I will protect my basic human rights.

◊ Since the new mindset that I have adopted empowers me to remain calm, secure, and resilient, I become enabled to regain my personal power and commit to the following ways of protecting and defending my personal rights:

» I will establish a set of appropriate and healthy personal boundaries that are founded on sound principles, such as compassion, logical reasoning, and wisdom.

» I will define and communicate these limits with Person D in a clear, firm, and respectful manner.

» When Person D violates my boundaries, I will hold them accountable by expressing myself openly, directly, gently, non-reactively, and non-provocatively. (See Appendix 1: *Assertive Communications*.)

» To preserve my personal integrity and effect change in Person D, I will maintain my personal boundary firmly, consistently, and constructively. (See Appendix 2: *Personal Boundary*.)

» Rather than enabling or criticizing Person D, I will support and empower them on their journey of transformation: When they make positive changes, I will offer genuine compliments and show my appreciation; when they return to their old unhealthy patterns of behaviors, I will:
  - Acknowledge my role in creating the problem (i.e., my own wrongdoing), offer my genuine apology, and commit to making positive changes;
  - Enlighten (i.e., share my feelings and thoughts in a gentle, respectful and healthy manner);
  - Set appropriate limits or consequences; and,
  - Follow through with the consequences consistently and firmly, but kindly.

» I realize that acceptance, empathy, and forgiveness does not mean that I stick by and get hurt time and time again. Therefore, I will commit to living a proactive life: I will consider the option A (i.e., cutting off) if my own true transformation does not bring about a change in Person D's behaviors. I understand that, in such a situation as this, Person D may have remained unawakened (i.e., lacks the awareness to understand how their behaviors make me feel). Naturally then, they would continue to behave in a harmful manner during setbacks or times of stress. Thus, I will forgive Person D, but I will not stand by and get hurt again—I will stay strong and cut off because I deserve to live a life with dignity and respect.

» When my basic human rights are violated by those who take sides (i.e., people whom Person D badmouths me to),

I will stay secure and separate: *"What others think of me is not for me to own."* While remaining non-judgmental and non-reactive, I will express myself in order to enlighten, not to criticize them or smear Person D.

» In addition to committing to these new learnings, I will revisit the unresolved issues from the past (by seeking professional help if I need to) in order to gain emotional healing (Table 12 on Page 143). I realize that healing the past wounds is essential for achieving total wellness.

» Finally, I understand that the true transformation is not about how often I face setbacks and regress to my old ways of being. Rather, it is about gaining resilience: How soon can I regain my inner control and change my thoughts and self-talks? How soon can I overcome my feelings of resentment and find the right path to a state of equanimity?

» In sum, I have arrived at the following conclusions:
  • Acknowledging my feelings and identifying with my own mind empowers me to remain secure and strong.
  • Empathizing with the feelings of others frees me from seeing myself as a victim and empowers me to remain calm and non-reactive.
  • When I use my Stop Sign (i.e., Stop, Think, and Act), I gain the ability to access these insights and protect my basic human rights in an effective way.

» Now, I am empowered to learn from my past mistakes, overcome my feelings of resentment, protect my basic human rights, and lead a more fulfilling life.

In summary, when we change our faulty ways of thinking by adopting sound principles that support self-compassion and fosters a positive self-image and sense of identity ("*I matter . . . I'm worthy*"), then we will be empowered to stay secure, strong, and separate in our relationships; protect and defend ourselves in a healthy and effective manner; and experience a sense of inner harmony and total wellness.

Table 12

Emotional Healing

Emotional healing is a process that takes place over time. When we reach a state of complete emotional well-being, then we are able to replace our feelings of resentment with a sense of calmness and equanimity. This is when we become enabled to learn from our past mistakes and make steady progress towards personal growth and total wellness.

The most important step that we may need to take in achieving emotional healing is forgiveness—forgiving our own past wrongdoings and extending this forgiveness towards those who have wronged us.

True and lasting forgiveness follows naturally after we gain awareness and achieve clarity: when we attain a deeper understanding into ourselves and others. Thus, adopting an empathic mindset may be the key to forgiveness.

Being able to forgive ourselves and others for our wrongdoings is freeing and empowering: As we no longer spend our time ruminating over grievances, we become empowered to lead a proactive life (i.e., learn from our mistakes, commit to new ways of being, and experience rewarding relationships).

Moreover, emotional healing improves our physical health by lowering the cortisol levels in our blood.

Perhaps then, it may make sense to even forgive those who may not deserve our forgiveness—since, we deserve to experience all that forgiveness and emotional healing offers us (i.e., total wellness).

"Holding on to anger is like grasping a hot coal with the intent of throwing it at someone else; you are the one who gets burned."—Buddha

To begin the process of true forgiveness and attain a true state of emotional healing, refer to <u>The Inner Control is the True Control Workbook, 2nd Edition</u>.

Mindfulness Scripts

> *Please pause a moment, take a few slow and deep breaths, and then read this script aloud.*

Naturally, in the early years of my childhood, I looked to my parents for protection. However, they were unable to protect me or help me feel safe or secure since they had limited *internal resources* (i.e., they weren't equipped with the skills to even protect their own basic human rights in a constructive manner).

As a result, I didn't learn what healthy personal boundaries were or how to set and maintain them in my relationships so that I could protect myself in an effective way.

Consequently, I transitioned into adulthood ill-equipped and unprepared to defend myself when my basic human rights were violated.

Perceiving myself as a victim, I felt helpless and trapped and therefore I wallowed in self-pity when I was wronged.

My self-discovery liberates me because it offers me the clarity to see *Me* and the inner resources that I naturally possess: now, I can see that I'm not stuck, nor am I helpless.

Now, I realize that I matter; I am worthy of being loved, protected, and taken care of.

Now, I understand that, as a mature adult, it is my responsibility to protect myself.

Now, I'm aware that I have the ability to lead a proactive life and guard my basic human rights.

Now, I *believe* that I am capable of learning constructive ways to set and maintain my personal boundaries and protect myself in a healthy way.

> *Please stay in the present moment!*

> *Please pause a moment, take a few slow and deep breaths, and then read this script aloud.*

Now that I have gained a sense of inner control and feel more secure and confident, I will live my life being unafraid of other people's:

> Angry or retaliatory responses or,
> their judgment, rejection, or abandonment.

Now that I am aware and mindful of my healthy personal boundaries, I will stay emotionally separate and express my feelings, thoughts, and observations in an assertive, appropriate, and respectful manner.

Now, I will maintain a relaxed posture, use a gentle tone of voice, and make eye contact that projects strength, confidence, and kindness.

Now, I can reach and maintain a state of equanimity.

> *Please stay in the present moment!*

> *Please pause a moment, take a few slow and deep breaths, and then read this script aloud.*

Now that I have gained a better understanding of healthy personal boundaries, I realize that I may have violated others' basic human rights in the past.

However, I also know that, before undertaking the journey of personal growth, I was emotionally stuck in my childhood; therefore, I didn't know any better.

Moreover, the insight that I have attained on the path to equanimity and personal growth enables me to see that imperfections is a human phenomenon.

Now, I realize that my mistakes do not define or devalue me, as a person.

As I understand the past and accept my humanness, I become empowered to forgive myself for my past wrong-doings.

Although I accept and forgive myself, I will not condone my maladaptive patterns of behaviors.

Now, I will reject *my faulty ways of thinking, feeling, and behaving*—not *Me*.

Now, I will hold myself accountable for my past mistakes: I will express regret and offer apologies in a sincere manner.

Now, I will lead a proactive and responsible life: I will commit to new learnings.

> *Please pause a moment and take a few slow and deep breaths before continuing to read this script aloud.*

My self-discovery humbles me and enables me to relate to other people's humanness: As humans, others cannot be perfect either.

I understand that, like me, people have learned their flawed ways of thinking, feeling, and behaving during their years of childhood.

As I gain insight into others and accept their humanness, I become empowered to forgive those who have crossed my boundaries and violated my basic human rights.

However, I realize that accepting and forgiving others does not mean that I condone their wrongdoings towards me; Acceptance and forgiveness does not mean that I stick by or go back and get hurt over and over again.

Now, I will:

Empathize with my own feelings;
Set healthy personal boundaries in my relationships;
and,
Hold others accountable consistently, firmly, respectfully, and appropriately.

Now, I will lead a proactive life.

> *Please pause a moment and take a few slow and deep breaths before continuing to read this script aloud.*

Now, I will allow the understanding mindset that I cultivated on the path to equanimity to help me open my heart to my parents.

Now,

I will extend my acceptance and
forgiveness to them:

I understand that, as imperfect human beings, my parents could have never been perfect people or perfect parents.

I realize that, like me, my parents learned many of their faulty ways of thinking, feeling, and behaving during the early years of their lives.

As I gain insight into my parents and accept their humanness, I become enabled to forgive them for their past wrongdoings and shortcomings towards me:

My parents were emotionally stuck in their childhood;
therefore, they didn't know any better.

Now,

I forgive my parents for all of the things that
I have blamed and resented them for.

Now,

I reject my parents' character flaws, not them.

Forgiveness heals me and allows me to
release my deep emotional pain.

Now, I don't need to tell others grievance stories and blame my parents for my present problems.

Part III - Chapter Seven

Now,

I understand that, as a mature adult,
I am responsible for my own ways of
thinking, feeling, or behaving.

Although I now accept and forgive my parents, I realize that forgiveness does not mean that I condone, justify, or excuse their wrongdoings or shortcomings towards me.

Now, I will lead a proactive life.

> *Please stay in the present moment!*

Why do we choose to enable others in our immediate environment?

Have we given up on ourselves or have we given up on them?

Source: <u>A Tool for Letting Go of Resentment and Anger: Short. Straightforward. Transformative.</u>

We use avoidance coping because we think that we are stuck. We are not; we have choices.

Source: <u>A Tool for Letting Go of Resentment and Anger: Short. Straightforward. Transformative.</u>

PART III - CHAPTER SEVEN

> *We get stuck on our journey when we focus on fixing others' flaws instead of focusing on improving those of our own.*

> *When we focus on changing others, we are fighting a losing battle.*

> *Retake your personal power and see your choices.*

> *While we cannot change people, we CAN support and empower them to grow and reach their full potential.*
>
> *To do so, we need to be strong and stay true to ourselves and others.*
>
> *When people are ready to deal with reality, they will face it and embark on their own journey of transformation.*

*Believe in yourself and live without fear;
Just allow the truth that you express to come
from the compassion in your heart.*

*Believe in others; As human beings,
no one is a fixed entity.*

Source: <u>A Tool for Letting Go of Resentment and Anger</u>:
<u>Short. Straightforward. Transformative</u>.

PART III - CHAPTER SEVEN

> *Always speak the truth. When people gain awareness and transform, they will remember you with gratitude.*

What is "empathy?"

Empathy is understanding why others think, feel, or behave the way they do.

This understanding comes from the compassion in our heart and is filtered through the thinking brain in our head.

In other words, empathy is accepting others' humanness without pitying them or condoning their hurtful behaviors.

Moreover, empathy is a prerequisite for achieving lasting forgiveness.

True forgiveness is a prerequisite for experiencing a genuine state of inner harmony and equanimity.

However, understanding and accepting others' humanness and forgiving them for their wrongdoings towards us does not mean that we stick by and get hurt time and time again.

*In sum, empathy is
an essential ingredient for emotional healing
and
a key for living a life free of emotional pain.*

PART III - CHAPTER SEVEN

"Forgiveness is giving up all hope of a better past." —Jack Kornfeld

While such measures as meditation, counseling, or anger-management training could bring about a sense of calmness, in the absence of true forgiveness, they may not result in a lasting emotional healing.

Source: <u>The Inner Control is the True Control Workbook, 2nd Edition</u>

Nothing may help us feel more grounded than facing our own humanness.

Nothing may help us forgive more readily than accepting other people's humanness.

Source: <u>The Inner Control is the True Control Workbook, 2nd Edition</u>

Retake Your Personal Power

1. Start on your journey of emotional growth by, first, understanding the past. This will help you forgive and let go of your resentments.
2. Then, search deep within you, discover your True Self, nurture it, and love yourself unconditionally.
3. Next, change the way you think and perceive reality. This will empower you to stand tall and hold your ground.
4. Here comes the most difficult part: Know that when your dearest loved ones feel threatened, rejected, or abandoned by your transformation, they may use their conditioned coping mechanisms (i.e., triangulation, shaming, guilting . . .) to get you back to where they can gain a sense of normalcy. Stay separate, secure, and strong but understand their experiences and empathize with their feelings. "They are hurting!" So, love the person they are but take issue with their ways of expressing themselves. This will empower them to grow with you.
5. Now, this may be the key to your success: Create a healthy environment for yourself that is conducive to growth. This means that you may have to cut yourself off from those who have held you back because they have resisted facing their own character flaws . . .
6. Finally, keep in mind that regression to old ways is a part of the process of change.
7. Now, as the saying goes: "Be proud of your scars and that you're still standing."

Emotional Self-Care: Listen to your Inner 'Self'

When we finally become strong and "choose" to cut off from those who resist facing their own character flaws, we are not abandoning them or causing them harm.

In such a time as this, cutting off is about "survival" and emotional self-care. This is so because we are listening to our Inner Child that says: "I have reached my limits and can no longer stick around and get hurt again and again. I have tried my best. It's time to take action. Please help me!"

Our Inner Child's reality is as real and as valid as that of others that we have to cut off from: "We matter!"

"You matter!"

Choose your environment carefully: People who are more aware, will not judge you; Instead, they will help, support, and empower you to leave destructive relationships when you are at the weakest point in your life and struggle to deal with your feelings of self-doubt, guilt, and inner conflict.

> *Surround yourself with those who will bring out the best in you.*

PART III - CHAPTER SEVEN

> *Work on staying secure, non-reactive, and understanding while remaining separate and strong in your relationship with your loved ones.*
>
> *Your transformation will not only help you live a more fulfilled life but also empower them to change and become the best version of themselves.*

> *Staying Non-Reactive ≠ Leading a Passive Life*

An Overview of the Mindsets that Lead to Harboring Resentment			
I have unrealistic expectations of myself ↓ I become hypersensitive to other people's negative but honest feedback or remarks ↓ I easily become offended	I have unrealistic expectations of others ↓ I become intolerant of people's certain way of thinking, feeling, or behaving ↓ I easily become annoyed	I need to be better than other people ↓ I constantly compare myself with others and become intolerant of people whom I perceive as superior or better than me ↓ I easily become jealous	I see other people as more worthy ↓ I over-function and become overly compliant, conciliatory, and enabling in my relationships with others ↓ I become an easy target for others
I Feel Offended!	**I Feel Annoyed!**	**I Feel Jealous!**	**I Feel Hurt!**

> *Just imagine a world where there is no resentment. In that world, we all choose to make better choices because we have gained awareness and replaced our unconscious trauma responses with well-thought-out coping strategies.*

PART IV

Conclusion

8

A Conscientious and Empowering Mindset

In Part I, we worked through the four steps of the genuine accountability process in order to take control of our lives and deal with our painful emotions during times of stress.

In doing so, we found answers to such questions as: "What are my feelings? How am I perceiving the stressful situation that I'm faced with? What are my internal thoughts and self-talks? How am I coping with the unpleasant realities and emotions that are generated by the way I'm perceiving this event? Am I using healthy coping strategies to deal with my feelings and resolve the problem? Or, could it be that I'm engaging in maladaptive behaviors (e.g., blaming, emotional eating, or drinking) in order to avoid facing the issue? What are the consequences of my action or inaction? Does my behavioral response play a part in my emotional suffering? How could I overcome my painful feelings and resolve the issue in such a way that would lead to inner peace and better outcomes? What are my choices? Do I see possibilities?"

The following summarizes how, in the hypothetical case studies presented in Part 1, we overcame our painful emotional experience (i.e., resentment) and regained our personal power through the process of genuine accountability:

We identified, acknowledged, and owned the negative emotions that we were feeling through self-observation (a non-judgmental manner of gaining self-awareness).

As we connected with our *Self* on a deeper level, we learned about our deep-seated emotions, internal thoughts, and self-talks.

We made sense of the insights that we gained into ourselves and discovered what happened: Our faulty ways of thinking had generated our feelings of resentment.

Through the process of observation (a non-judgmental manner of gaining awareness into other people), we came to uncover another truth: our maladaptive coping strategies had a fundamental role in our emotional suffering.

While holding ourselves accountable, we accepted our humanness and forgave ourselves for our wrongdoings.

Our self-discoveries and self-compassion empowered us to relate to others' experiences, accept their humanness, and forgive them for their wrongdoings towards us.

Feeling liberated from emotional anguish, we were able to reach emotional healing, learn from our past mistakes, and commit to new ways of being.

Our transformation empowered us to remain calm, secure, separate, reflective, and proactive in the face of adversity.

Since we had gained the ability to retake our inner control and retain our personal power in times of stress, we were able to see new possibilities, make better choices (Appendix 3), and experience less emotional pain and negative outcomes.

In short, Part 1 established that we could overcome our feelings of resentment and reach a state of equanimity when we look inwardly (to face our own character flaws) rather than look outwardly (to change or fix other people's flaws).

Moreover, Part 1 showed us that the insight, knowledge, and wisdom that we attain as a result of working through this process help us reach our full potential: Our gained insight, knowledge, and wisdom will empower us to develop and cultivate a set of healthy values, beliefs, and standards. These sound principles will build the foundation for a conscientious and empowering mindset. Such a constructive state of mind will:

◊ Support a positive attitude towards our self and help us build a strong sense of our value and worth, as a person;

◊ Foster a positive attitude towards others and help us form rewarding relationships;

◊ Motivate us to learn from our mistakes and commit to our new ways of being (i.e., thinking, feeling, and behaving);

◊ Empower us to make well-thought-out decisions that are morally right and result in positive outcomes;

◊ Help us build resilience and find equanimity in the face of adversity; and,

◊ Enable us to improve our overall well-being: As we build resilience and gain the ability to effectively manage our setbacks and relapses (i.e., regressions to our old ways of being), we will become empowered to engage in a more consistent self-care, stick to our healthy lifestyle changes, reach our goals (e.g., maintain our weight loss or sobriety), and enjoy better physical and emotional health.

Thus, we may conclude that working through the four steps of the process genuine accountability is *empowering* (i.e., it empowers us to transform); *liberating* (i.e., it frees us from experiencing emotional pain); and, *inspiring* (i.e., it inspires other people to gravitate towards us, change, and find inner peace).

PART IV - CHAPTER EIGHT

> *How awakened am I?*
> *Do I shape my environment?*
> *Or, does my environment shape the*
> *way I think, feel, and behave?*

> *It takes courage to grow up
> and become who you really are.*
> —E.E.Cummings

9

Conscientious and Empowering Inner Thoughts and Self-Talks

As discussed earlier in this book, when we remain unaware and live on autopilot, our negative emotional experiences may trigger faulty patterns of internal thoughts and dialogues that were programmed in us during the early years of our lives.

In such situations, our conditioned mindset drives a set of automatic and maladaptive behaviors, such as avoidance coping, to help us deal with our emotional pain (e.g., we may drink or eat to soothe our feelings of resentment).

Therefore, in times of stress, we may struggle to stick to our healthy behavioral and lifestyle changes and reach total wellness.

Moreover, as was explained in Chapter 2, chronic stress leads to prolonged elevation of cortisol levels in our blood, which in turn, can cause physical, emotional, and mental health problems.

Thus, gaining control over our lives and overcoming our negative emotional experiences (i.e., resentment) is essential in reaching a state of total wellness.

This final chapter emphasizes the importance of genuine self-accountability (i.e., being aware and accountable to ourselves) in achieving this state of physical, mental, and emotional well-being.

Through offering a set of conscientious and empowering self-dialogues (below), this section reviews how, in the hypothetical case studies presented in Chapters 4 through 7, we were enabled to overcome our feelings of resentment when we cultivated sound principles and changed our mindset.

These internal self-talks will empower us to stay committed to our healthy behavioral and lifestyle changes, reach our goals, and maintain our total well-being even when we are faced with adversity.

My Conscientious and Empowering Internal Dialogues

Now that I'm more awakened,
I will face the truth.

Now,
When I experience resentment, I will accept that:
I cannot change or fix anyone.

This acceptance is 'not' an act of passivity;
Rather, it is an act of proactivity:

Seeing and accepting others the way they are will enable me to refocus and redirect my attention to the areas of my life that I have control over.

Therefore, now,
When I experience resentment,
I will focus on my own part: my wrongdoings.

Now,
I will acknowledge the emotions that I feel by observing my 'self' and asking:

Am I offended?
Am I Annoyed?
Am I Jealous? Or,
Am I wronged?

Owning my feelings will help me become self-aware and discover my mistakes (my maladaptive coping strategy).

I now realize that my own reactions are what I can control.

Now,
I will take ownership of my flawed ways of thinking that drive my reactions.

As I hold myself accountable for the consequences of my behavioral responses, I will gain the ability to hold onto my personal power and stay in control of my life.

Therefore, now,
I will commit to changing my flaws:

I will improve my ways of coping with my negative emotions by allowing the Nurturing Adult within me to govern my internal thoughts and dialogues.

This constructive state of mind will generate positive feelings and drive healthy behaviors and coping strategies.

Now,
I will be proactive:

I will establish a set of healthy personal boundaries that fits the more awakened Me.

I will protect my basic human rights by maintaining these boundaries consistently and appropriately.

*While I stay separate and preserve my individuality,
I will be understanding towards the feelings and
experiences of others.*

*Moreover, I will respect people's personal boundaries
as I wish others to respect mine—because, we all
deserve to be treated with dignity.*

Now,

*I will let go of my feelings of resentment and commit
to my new learnings:*

*When I'm offended, I will own my feelings and find inner
peace by re-evaluating the way I perceive reality.*

*When I'm annoyed, I will own my feelings and find inner
peace by setting limits with myself: "The feelings, thoughts,
and the choices that others make belong to them."*

*When I'm jealous, I will own my feelings and find inner peace by
allowing the Nurturing Parent within me to affirm me; and,*

*When I'm wronged, I will own my feelings and find
inner peace by setting healthy limits with those who have
violated my basic human rights: "It is on me to protect
and maintain my personal boundaries."*

Now, I understand that,
*Human development is a continual process;
It starts at birth and ends when we die.*

*As long as we live and interact with the environment (i.e., other
people), we will continue to transform.*

Therefore, I, like others, will always be a work in progress.

*Accepting that I am not special and can never
be perfect liberates me: Now, I can forgive
myself for my past mistakes.*

*Accepting that other people can never be perfect
empowers me: Now, I can be more tolerant
and forgiving of others' mistakes.*

Forgiveness gives me the power to heal.

Therefore, now,
I will let go of the past hurts.

Now, I realize that,
*The more resilient I become,
the more I can feel my emotions;*

*The more empathy I cultivate,
the more deeply and intensely
I can feel these emotions.*

Therefore, now,
*I will learn healthy coping strategies, such as channeling,
to reach a state of equanimity.*

*For example,
I will direct my feelings of jealousy into positive actions
(i.e., I will empower myself to make better choices)
in order to achieve my goals and aspirations;*

Or,

*I will direct my hurt feelings into positive actions (i.e., I will
enlighten, support, and empower others to find equanimity
and emotional healing) in order to heal myself.*

Finally, now,
I will stay confident and emotionally independent.

*I will do what is right and what is kind—not
what is customary or what is nice.*

*I will create a positive and healthy environment for
myself and engage in responsible self-care.*

I will set goals and come up with a plan of actions.

*When I am faced with a difficult situation, I will
face and accept the truth: I cannot change anyone;
however, I can change and effect change.*

Therefore, now,
*When I am faced with a difficult situation,
I will become self-aware; understand what happened;
hold myself accountable for my mistakes; and,
commit to new learnings.*

Now,
While I remain hopeful, I will be realistic:

*When I stay committed,
I can reach my goals.*

Part IV - Chapter Nine

> *We will effect change and reap the rewards when we do what is kind that is right—even when it's hard.*

> *"Believe in yourself; Believe in everyone.*
> *Become enlightened by gaining insight.*
> *Enlighten others by expressing yourself.*
> *Your journey together is* effecting change together."
>
> Source: <u>Building a Strong Sense of Self</u>:
> <u>Embarking on the Journey of Change</u>

APPENDIX

APPENDIX: 1

ASSERTIVE COMMUNICATIONS

When we no longer need to be affirmed or acknowledged by others to feel good or worthy, we become liberated and empowered to be true to ourselves and other people.

In such a state of high confidence, we will be able to remain self-assured, emotionally independent, and authentic. Thus, we will not communicate in a passive, aggressive, or passive-aggressive way; rather, we will express ourselves and maintain our personal boundaries in an assertive and effective manner.

The following outlines some of the key components of assertive communications:

- » We express our thoughts, feelings, wishes, and needs:
    - Directly (without involving other people);
    - Non-reactively and non-provocatively;
    - Straightforwardly, clearly, openly, and sincerely—without premeditation;
    - Firmly and respectfully; and,
    - In a calm, friendly, and gentle tone of voice.
- » We use "I" statements: *"I felt B when you did A."*
- » We listen without interrupting.
- » We make eye contact and maintain a relaxed posture.
- » We address issues and problems as they arise.
- » We make choices that are based on sound principles, such as wisdom, logical reasoning, free will, and virtues of love and humanity.

- » We honor our words and make trustworthy commitments because our decisions are based on free will, and not fear (i.e., fear of others' judgment, rejection, abandonment or angry reactions).
- » We take responsibility for our mistakes and offer sincere apologies.
- » We are self-aware and express our true feelings, opinions, and desires since we know that we matter.
- » We are true to others and speak our mind because we not only believe in other people but also respect and care enough about them to tell them the truth.
- » We make requests (i.e., *"Would you please . . ."*) and not demand (i.e., *"Stop! . . . You need to . . . You should . . . I want you to . . . I need you to . . ."*).
- » We treat everyone (children, the elderly, the disabled, minorities, the poor, or the unhoused) with respect and integrity.

In sum, we communicate in a manner by which it conveys such a message as this:

> *"I will treat you the way I would like [and deserve] to be treated by you — with respect and integrity."*

APPENDIX: 2

PERSONAL BOUNDARY

Naturally, a boundary is a line that indicates a limit where two entities become different; as a result, these two entities remain separate within their respective border line.

Accordingly, a personal boundary is a metaphor that is applied to a point at which two mature adults become *two different entities*; as a result, each individual stays within their own respective physical, emotional, mental, spiritual, material, and sexual space.

For example, as mature adults, our thoughts, feelings, opinions, and hopes; the way we express our feelings; the choices we make in our lives; and, the food we put in our mouth are all entities that remain within our imaginary border line.

In other words, when people in a group maintain their healthy personal boundaries, each person has a right to their own ways of thinking, feeling, and behaving. Accordingly, each individual in the group is responsible for his or her attitude, emotions, and actions.

Defining, setting, and maintaining a set of healthy personal boundaries is a learned behavior. Becoming aware and mindful of our basic personal rights is vital in having healthy and rewarding relationships.

Being mindful of our own personal boundaries enables us to respect those of others: our mindfulness helps us understand that when we cross people's boundaries without their full consent, we are invading and violating their basic personal rights and causing emotional pain. This awareness empowers us to hold ourselves accountable for our actions.

Additionally, being mindful of our personal boundaries enables us to have more self-respect and lead a proactive life: our mindfulness helps us understand that when people cross our boundaries, then we are responsible for holding them accountable for their actions.

Finally, self-awareness helps us realize that we may not have healthy personal boundaries (i.e., we are not setting *clear* limits or we are not *honoring* the limits that we set with others) when our lines are crossed and our basic personal rights are violated *time after time*. (For setting and maintaining healthy personal boundaries, refer to the forthcoming book: *The ABC's of Healthy Personal Boundaries*.)

In sum:

> » As mature adults, it is *our* responsibility to establish, set, and maintain our healthy boundaries.

> » Respecting and honoring others' personal boundaries stops us from being self-righteous, judgmental, punishing, and controlling.

> » Setting clear limits with other people and maintaining them firmly, consistently, respectfully, and appropriately protect us from being controlled, manipulated, punished, and victimized by others.

> » Lastly, establishing, setting and maintaining healthy personal boundaries in our relationships empowers us to stay secure and harbor such constructive internal thoughts and dialogues as: *"What other people think of me is not for me to own . . . Rather than worrying about what others think of me, I will ask myself: How do my behaviors make people feel?"*

APPENDIX: 3

A CHECKLIST FOR MAKING BETTER CHOICES

As discussed earlier in this book, working through the process of genuine accountability not only helps us overcome our emotional pain but also (by providing a framework) enables us to make optimal decisions and resolve our problems.

An optimal decision may be defined as an informed choice that can be carried out consistently since it is formed based on solid facts (knowledge) and sound principles (wisdom).

The decisions that are made by such a knowledgeable and principled mindset will naturally result in better outcomes and less negative consequences (i.e., we will live a more fulfilled life and experience less depressed moods).

Through offering a checklist that is designed based on such a decision-making model, this section will guide the reader to solve problems and make better choices.

Table 13, on the next page, provides an overview of this model.

Table 13

A Decision-Making Model

1. **Identify**:
   Define the issue at hand.

2. **Gather Information**:
   Obtain thorough, valid, and reliable information (*the fact*) that is available to you on this matter—This information is *"reality."*

3. **Become Knowledgeable**:
   Educate yourself and make sense of the information that you have collected—Your knowledge of the fact is *"your reality."*

4. **Develop Wisdom**:
   » Reflect on what you have learned.
   » Interpret, analyze, reason, filter, and extract the knowledge that is logical, feasible, and realistic.
   » Establish a clear thought process based on this knowledge: find clarity and put things into perspective.
   » Form and adopt a set of sound principles (i.e., *solid beliefs*)—This is the bedrock of a *consistent and steady mindset*.
   » Your insight and understanding of the knowledge that you have gained is *"your truth."*

5. **Consider Options:**
   » By using the knowledge and wisdom that you have gained, make a list of all the possible choices that are available to you.
   » Weigh your options and identify the potential consequences that may be associated with each one.

6. **Make a Decision:**
   » Choose the option that has the best outcomes and the least negative consequences.

7. **Act and Commit:**
   » Act on your decision to meet your target—This is your *goal*.
   » Make and carry out a realistic plan of action by taking small but steady steps to achieve your goal.

Table 13

A Decision-Making Model (Cont'd)

- » Be proactive: Anticipate and identify the possible events or setbacks that could stop you from staying committed to your plans.
- » Make a contingency plan to deal with these obstacles (i.e., come up with healthy and effective strategies for adjusting, adapting, or responding appropriately and effectively).
- » In the face of adversity, stay strong and stick to the plans that you have made.

Post Action: Evaluate and Enhance Wisdom: Evaluate the decision that you have made by assessing and appraising the outcomes:

- » List the positive outcomes, acknowledge your good choice, and build upon your success.
- » Face the negative consequences, admit that you have made a poor choice, hold yourself accountable for your mistakes, and direct your focus onto finding the root cause.
- » Gain more wisdom by learning from your mistakes.
- » Commit to your new learnings in order to avoid making the same mistakes—This is the key to *staying consistent and continually making better decisions*.

Throughout your decision-making experiences, support yourself and maintain your inner control by having self-nurturing internal dialogues:

- » *I will always try to make the best choice possible.*
- » *In case of adversity (negative outcomes), I will face, own, and deal with the natural feelings of regret.*
- » *I realize that as a human being, I am bound to make mistakes. I will look at those mistakes as an opportunity for growth and a better tomorrow.*

Now, let us reframe our mindset and view a poor decision, failure, or setback as a stepping stone to success.

A Checklist for Making an Optimal Decision

1. Identify the problem:

☐ I'm contemplating this issue:

_____
_____
_____
_____
_____
_____
_____
_____
_____
_____
_____
_____
_____
_____
_____
_____
_____
_____
_____
_____
_____
_____
_____
_____
_____
_____

2. **Gather information:**

    ☐ Do I have all the relative and necessary information in regard to the issue at hand?

    ☐ Is this information valid? Is it reliable? Does it come from a credible source? (An information that has been passed on to us by the people in our environment, may be *others' truth* and not *the truth* (*the fact*). An example of this would be a trending diet versus a dietary guideline that is backed by *extensive* scientific evidence.)

    ☐ These are *the facts* that I have gathered about this issue:

    _____
    _____
    _____
    _____
    _____
    _____
    _____
    _____
    _____
    _____
    _____
    _____
    _____
    _____
    _____
    _____
    _____
    _____
    _____
    _____
    _____

3. **Become knowledgeable:**

    ☐ Do I understand and make sense of the information that I have collected?

    ☐ Have I learned enough about this matter to be able to make an informed decision?

    ☐ This is what I know (i.e., what I have learned) about the issue at hand (*my reality*):

    _____
    _____
    _____
    _____
    _____
    _____
    _____
    _____
    _____
    _____
    _____
    _____
    _____
    _____
    _____
    _____
    _____
    _____
    _____
    _____
    _____
    _____
    _____
    _____
    _____

4. Develop wisdom:

☐ Have I reflected on what I have learned?

☐ Have I sorted out and analyzed what I have learned in order to extract the knowledge that is real and sound?

☐ In other words, is my reality real? Is the knowledge that I have gained the truth (i.e., a belief that is formed based on facts) and not a distorted reality (i.e., a false belief that is formed to support *what I want to believe*)?

☐ Can I now see things more clearly?

☐ Can I put things into perspective?

☐ Do I now have a clear thought process?

☐ This is what I believe about this issue based on what I have learned (*my truth*):

_____
_____
_____
_____
_____
_____
_____
_____
_____
_____
_____
_____
_____
_____
_____
_____
_____
_____

5. Consider options:

☐ Have I explored all the options that are available to me in order to deal with this matter?

☐ This is a list of the choices that I have made:

_____
_____
_____
_____
_____
_____
_____
_____
_____
_____
_____
_____
_____
_____
_____
_____
_____
_____
_____
_____
_____
_____
_____
_____
_____
_____
_____
_____
_____
_____

- [ ] Have I weighed these options? Have I analyzed the pros and cons of each choice?

- [ ] These are the possible negative consequences of each of the options that I have listed above:

6. **Make a decision:**

☐ Have I chosen the option that results in a more positive outcome (i.e., has the least negative consequences)?

☐ Is this choice based on sound principles (a principled mindset) so that I could stay committed to my decision? To put it differently, is my decision:

☐ Realistic, practical, and feasible?

☐ Based on a *choice* that comes from my heart (the thinking brain) and not a *reaction* that comes from a place of resentment and anger (the emotional brain)?

☐ Responsible? Simply put, by choosing this option, will I be conscientious of others *and* myself? For instance, if I carry out this decision:
  ☐ Will I be true to myself?
  ☐ Will I be true to others?
  ☐ Will I be respectful of the basic human rights of other people?
  ☐ Will my choice be based on my own free will and not out of fear of other people's judgment, rejection, or abandonment (because I need to please others and gain their approval)?
  ☐ Will my choice be based on my own free will and not out of fear of other people's angry or retaliatory reactions (because I see myself as a weak and helpless individual)?
  ☐ Will I be striking a *balance*? In other words, will I be giving up the pleasure of the Now for the gratification of tomorrow when it is necessary for me to do so? (This Moment—the Now—is important because it is the one part of our lives that we can control: the past has past and the future is not here. Although tomorrow is uncertain, science has shown us that we can make predictions about it based on the events of today. As a result, today, we can act in such a way

to gain *more* control of the future—the unknown. Therefore, while the pleasure of this moment is *vital* in experiencing a sense of emotional well-being, making a decision that takes the future's possible outcomes into account is *equally* essential: Clearly, our rash or not well-thought-out choices can negatively impact the Moments of tomorrow.)

☐ This is my final decision:

_____
_____
_____
_____
_____
_____
_____
_____
_____
_____
_____
_____
_____
_____
_____
_____
_____
_____
_____
_____

7. Act and commit:

☐ Do I have an action plan that will hold me accountable and help me stay committed to this decision?

☐ This is how I will carry out my decision (my action plan):

In order to set myself up for success, I will make realistic and achievable plans: ___

☐ These are the possible events or obstacles that may prevent me from sticking to my decision?

☐ This is how I would deal with events or setbacks (i.e., negative outcomes) that could stop me from staying committed to my decision (i.e., adjust, adapt, or respond appropriately and effectively):

APPENDIX THREE

POST ACTION

Evaluate and enhance wisdom:

☐ These are the positive outcomes of my decision:

☐ These are the negative consequences of my decision:

Appendix Three

☐ These are the mistakes that I made:

☐ This may be the root cause of my mistakes:

☐ This is what I would do differently the next time:

☐ This is what I have learned from this experience:

"Just as one candle lights another and can light thousands of other candles, so one heart illuminates another heart and can illuminate thousands of other hearts."

Source: *A Calendar of Wisdom by Leo Tolstoy*

References

Gilbert, Roberta (1992). *Extraordinary Relationships: A New Way of Thinking About Human Interactions*. Minneapolis, MN: Chronimed Publishing.

Luskin, Fred (2009). *Forgive for Love: The Missing Ingredient for a Healthy and Lasting Relationship*. New York, NY: HarperCollins Publishers.

Ruiz, Don Miguel (1997). *The Four Agreements*. San Rafael, CA: Amber-Allen Publishing.

Seligman, Martin (2002). *Authentic Happiness*. New York, NY: Free Press.

Shannon, Joseph (2016). *Understanding Personality Disorders* [Audio-Visual DVD]. USA: Institute for Brain Potential.

Vander Zanden, James (1978). *Human Development*. New York, NY: Random House.

Index

Aha Moment	37
All-or-None Attitude	89
Aggressive	12, 115, 131, 134, 187
Assertive	30, 139, 147, 187
Awakened	13, 26, 27, 29, 30, 127, 173, 176, 177
Boundaries	30, 49, 65, 74, 87, 90, 93, 98, 100, 130, 133, 134, 136, 139, 145, 146, 147, 148, 149, 177, 178, 187, 189-190
Buddha	143
Character Traits	51, 71, 82, 93
Cortisol	33, 34, 143, 175
Decision-Making Model	191, 192, 193
Emotional Brain	102, 201
Emotional Healing	11, 14, 87, 121, 124, 141, 143, 144, 156, 157, 170, 179
Emotional Rights	123, 125, 130
Emotionally Dependent	133
Empathy	86, 112, 115, 134, 137, 140, 156, 179
Enlighten	11, 79, 140, 141, 179
Fact	191, 192, 195, 197
Forgiveness	139, 140, 143, 144, 149, 150, 151, 156, 157, 179

Genuine Accountability	7, 8, 23, 27, 32, 33, 35-40, 41, 42, 47, 48, 51, 71, 72, 78, 81, 85, 103, 107, 109, 110, 121, 122, 124, 129, 135, 169, 172, 191
Imperfection	56, 59, 81, 86, 90, 91, 114, 148
Individuality	130, 133, 178
Inner Control	5, 85, 100, 141, 147, 170, 193
Joseph Campbell	13
Knowledge	12, 36, 37, 48, 52, 57, 60, 72, 79, 98, 104, 107, 122, 130, 171, 191, 192, 193, 197
Leo Tolstoy	92
Material Rights	124
Obsessive-compulsive behaviors	84
Passive	88, 131, 134, 137, 161, 187
Passive-Aggressive	110, 115, 131, 134, 187
Passivity	20, 131, 132, 176
Perfection	17, 27, 28, 51, 56, 74, 81, 89, 91, 97, 114, 148
Perfectionism	89
Perfectionist	73
Perfectionistic	27, 89
Personal Boundaries	See Boundaries
Physical Rights	123
Prefrontal Cortex	57, 139
Regression	158, 171
Relapse	25, 26, 28, 171
Resilience	53, 87, 110, 111, 128, 141, 171

APPENDIX INDEX

Routine	76, 78, 82
Separate	86, 87, 138, 141, 142, 147, 158, 161, 170, 178, 189
Sexual Rights	124, 125
Spiritual Rights	124
State of Anxiety and inner turmoil	131, 132
State of Compliance	131, 132, 133
State of Passivity	131, 132
State of Reactivity	131, 132
State of Reconciliation	132, 133
State of Remorse	132, 133
Stress	7, 8, 23, 24, 25, 26, 28, 33, 34, 35, 36, 42, 51, 52, 53, 54, 77, 85, 92, 101, 102, 111, 123, 124, 127, 128, 130, 131, 135, 136, 137, 140, 169, 170, 171, 175
Thinking Brain	57, 139, 156, 201
Total Self	54, 85, 88, 111, 137, 138
Verbal Rights	123, 125
Wisdom	112, 139, 171, 187, 191, 192, 193, 197, 207

Living a Fulfilled Life

To achieve your goals, reach your dreams, and live a fulfilled life, *expand your knowledge, make sound decisions,* and *deal with setbacks* (a natural part of the process).

To expand your knowledge, **read**, don't just listen to podcasts or audiobooks: Reading is an active way of learning; It stimulates the parts of the brain that process visual information and foster creative, critical, and analytical thinking. On the other hand, listening may be a passive way of learning; It stimulates the auditory part of our brain, disrupts our thoughts, and redirects our focus; therefore, it may change or reinforce the way we think and feel about something.

We gain greater knowledge when we
maintain our proactivity, creativity and individuality.

To make sound decisions, **reflect and consider all your choices**, don't just react to a trigger or accept whatever you read or hear: The process of reflection takes place in the prefrontal cortex of the brain. This part of our brain regulates our emotions and impulses and helps us make choices that result in better outcomes.

We make better decisions when we
stop, think, and act.

To deal with a setback, **look inwardly to find answers and resolve the problem**, don't just blame or focus on other people's part in it: Self-accountability helps us stay in control and see choices, while blaming or focusing on other people's faults makes us feel frustrated and stuck.

"*It is far more useful to be aware of a single shortcoming in ourselves than it is to be aware of a thousand shortcomings in someone else. For when the fault is our own, we are in a position to correct it.*" —Dalai Lama

We manage setbacks more effectively when we
retain our personal power and stay in control of our lives.

Building a Strong Sense of Self: Embarking on the Journey of Change

Many of us know from experience that maintaining healthy habits is challenging: A minor change in our daily routine, caused by a stressful situation, can make us slip and return to our old patterns.

Building a Strong Sense of Self: Embarking on the Journey of Change helps us sustain our healthy behavioral and lifestyle changes regardless of the challenges we face.

This transformative book starts us on this journey by inspiring us to search deep within, discover our *Inner Self* (our *True Self*), and love our *Self* unconditionally.

As we go through this process, we come to cultivate a mindset that is rooted in such principles as *free will, logical reasoning, and compassion.* In times of stress, such a constructive mindset will guide our thoughts, drive our behaviors, and help us stick to our lifestyle modifications.

Since we are no longer enslaved to our old habits, we will *maintain* our behavioral changes, achieve our health goals, and experience rewarding outcomes.

This is how embarking on the journey of change will empower us to gain a sense of physical, emotional, and mental well-being (i.e., a state of total wellness).

Building a Strong Sense of Self: Embarking on the Journey of Change has received an unsolicited endorsement from a reputable licensed marriage and family counselor. In addition to empowering others to change their lifestyle, This book has helped couples and transformed many relationships.

www.ingramcontent.com/pod-product-compliance
Lightning Source LLC
Chambersburg PA
CBHW071352290426
44108CB00014B/1516